THE
DRAMATIC
DECADE

ADVANCE PRAISE FOR THE BOOK

'Pages from India's history written by the highest court have been brought together. It is a must-read for any citizen who wishes to understand how the Supreme Court has shaped the legal landscape of India'— P. Chidambaram, former Union finance minister

'*The Dramatic Decade* undertakes a deep analysis of the judgments that literally shook the nation and have had a resounding impact on the society as a whole. It is a testimony of faith in the apex institution in performing its role of safeguarding the rights and welfare of a population of over 1.3 billion. Indu Bhan has compiled this book with rich illustrations from the pages of history, and I am sure that it will be a useful addition to the library of lawyers, academicians, parliamentarians and society at large'—K.K. Venugopal, attorney general of India

'In one of the best plays of its time, in 1972, Tom Stoppard had one of his characters say: "This is a British murder inquiry and some degree of justice must be seen to be more or less done." Bhan's perceptive treatment of the twelve landmark cases of modern India successfully shows that in each of them "some degree of justice" was more or less done!'— Fali Nariman, constitutional expert and veteran lawyer

'Having had the benefit of reading Bhan's first book, *Legal Eagles*, I am convinced that only she can make a dry subject riveting, gripping, compelling, captivating and engaging. A must-read'—Tushar Mehta, additional solicitor general

'A thoughtful collection of significant cases in the last decade, from violence and tragedy to protection and triumph of rights. The narrative is engaging, eloquent and informative. Indeed a dramatic decade!'— Meenakshi Arora, senior Supreme Court lawyer

Foreword by Harish Salve

THE DRAMATIC DECADE

Landmark Cases of Modern India

Indu Bhan

PENGUIN
VIKING
An imprint of Penguin Random House

VIKING

USA | Canada | UK | Ireland | Australia
New Zealand | India | South Africa | China | Singapore

Viking is part of the Penguin Random House group of companies
whose addresses can be found at global.penguinrandomhouse.com

Published by Penguin Random House India Pvt. Ltd
4th Floor, Capital Tower 1, MG Road,
Gurugram 122 002, Haryana, India

Penguin
Random House
India

First published in Viking by Penguin Random House India 2017

10 9 8 7 6 5 4 3 2

The views and opinions expressed in this book are the author's own and the
facts are as reported by her which have been verifi ed to the extent possible,
and the publishers are not in any way liable for the same.

ISBN 9780670089291

Typeset in Adobe Caslon Pro by R. Ajith Kumar, New Delhi
Printed at Replika Press Pvt. Ltd, India

www.penguin.co.in

MIX
Paper from
responsible sources
FSC® C016779

This is a legitimate digitally printed version of the book and therefore might not
have certain extra finishing on the cover.

Contents

Contents

Foreword

The Indian Republic is now seventy. In these seven turbulent decades, its democracy has only grown stronger. Trials and tribulations were inevitable in the transition from a feudal and economically backward country—forged into a single unit of governance for the first time—to the world's largest democracy with the fastest-growing economy which aspires for a seat in the UN Security Council. That too in an era when countries around it failed as democracies. Our constitutional institutions have stood up to challenges and grown in strength and stature. They have also had their moments which shouldn't have been, but have shown the resilience to rebound.

One institution that has made its mark not just in India, but globally, and has redefined the role of the judiciary not only as an arbiter of disputes, but as an institution of constitutional governance, is the Supreme Court. Significant events in the journey of this democracy have had their resonance felt in the Supreme Court. This book talks about some of these events, and their judicial resonance, that marked the last decade, like the Mumbai attacks—and its aftermath in the courts. India resisted the temptation of resorting to a summary military tribunal to try a terrorist who was caught red-handed. He was given a fair trial, with the Supreme Court appointing an eminent counsel to appear as amicus curiae to argue the defence.

The book picks on the leading cases, not only for their jurisprudential worth, but also because they have marked the culmination of dramatic events in a logical conclusion fashioned by the rule of law. From cases arising out of the scourge of terrorism to those that have defined the reform in election laws and the growing recognition of gender justice—the list goes on.

The author has taken to becoming a historian of the Supreme Court, and I am sure that the generations that follow will be grateful for her efforts—students of law and those who follow current events will find her account to be of great interest. Even those of us who treat cases—big and small—as part of a day's work, would find this book interesting, for looking back at what we have traversed, the title of the book appears to be more than justified—truly, we have lived through a dramatic decade!

November 2017

Harish Salve
Former solicitor general of India and
senior lawyer

Introduction

This book is a modest attempt at highlighting some pertinent issues that have plagued our system and been a matter of debate in our society.

Capital punishment, rape laws, the issue of transgender and LGBT rights, the criminalization of politics and the freedom of speech are topics that are woven into the fabric of our society. These continue to have a profound effect on how we live and experience life. From time to time, some of these issues have been addressed by the courts. *The Dramatic Decade* is an attempt to offer a ringside view of these cases and judgments to the readers.

It is the three Cs—case, cause and concern—that have underpinned the structure of this book. The main sources for this book have been the court records for the cases that have progressed from lower courts to high courts and the Supreme Court, as well as media reports and the opinions of legal experts.

Introduction

The cases against Ajmal Kasab, Afzal Guru and Yakub Memon, for the Mumbai attacks, the Parliament attack and the Mumbai serial blasts, will offer the readers a peek into the volatile world of war. These were wars of a different kind. These cases brought back the debate on death penalty and made us think about its impact on the collective conscience of the nation.

> The world today is wild with the delirium of hatred,
> the conflicts are cruel and unceasing in anguish,
> crooked are its paths . . .
> Man's heart is anguished with the fever of unrest,
> with the poison of self-seeking,
> with a thirst that knows no end.

Today, one can see the relevance of these lines by Rabindranath Tagore.

Lily Thomas was seventy-eight when she decided to bring about a major change to usher in a clean political system. The repercussions were far and wide and several political stalwarts were debarred from contesting elections. Shreya Singhal was twenty-one when she became instrumental in bringing about a change in the IT Act in order to defend the freedom of speech.

Nirbhaya's is a heart-rending tale. The case that shook the entire nation was instrumental in bringing about amendments in rape laws.

When the LGBT community fought for its rights, it was a wake-up call for exhibiting tolerance and acceptance sans prejudice.

Introduction

The Uphaar tragedy is a reminder to take safety and security measures—it highlights how a lapse and lack of time-bound intervention can be tragic.

The controversy surrounding the Babri Masjid—an unending battle which started with the first incidence of religious violence in 1853—and its impact will give readers a sense of history.[1] The first civil suits were filed by both Hindus and Muslims in 1949.

The twists and turns of the Mumbai bar dancers case provide an insight into the vicissitudes of human emotions and values.

This is the spectrum that the book attempts to cover.

The Dramatic Decade is intended to inform and create awareness and does not aim to propagate any school of thought. Care has been taken not to besmirch the name of any person or community, and readers are called upon to read issues afresh.

If only we could look inwards, if only we could exhibit a reasonable amount of tolerance and acceptance ... the world would be a different place.

Change is inevitable and the issues presented in the book are likely to be addressed in a better way in due course. I have just initiated the process and hope to hit the chord of sensitivity that would help foster tolerance, acceptance and accommodation.

Time and space constraints may have compelled me to omit several issues and cases that would have embellished the saga of this dramatic decade. The omissions are not intentional.

To quote Francis Bacon, 'Studies serve for delight, for

ornament, and for ability . . . Some books are to be tasted, others to be swallowed, and some few to be chewed and digested.'

The Dramatic Decade is thus designed and structured to be a living testimony. It is a reminder to readers, and to all those who plan to enter the legal profession, to uphold what is right and just.

1

The Parliament Attack

Collective Conscience

'Tragedy is an imitation of an action that is serious, complete and of a certain magnitude ... with incidents arousing pity and fear ... bringing about a catharsis of these emotions.'

—Aristotle

It all started on 13 December 2001 at 11.35 a.m. A beacon-fitted white Ambassador with identity stickers of the Ministry of Home Affairs attempted to enter the Indian Parliament.

An alert Central Reserve Police Force (CRPF) constable Kamlesh Kumari got suspicious of the fast-moving vehicle when it entered through main iron gate no. 1 for VVIPs on Parliament Street. In no time, Kamlesh realized that there was a breach of security. She was the first person to spot the intruders. Armed with just a walkie-talkie, she screamed and alerted ward staff J.P. Yadav.

'*Yadav, gate bandh kar* [Yadav, close the gate],' she shouted as she ran towards the gate. Yadav, too, rushed to seal the gate.

Sensing that their entry would be blocked, the intruders started firing. They pumped eleven bullets into Kamlesh's stomach, killing her on the spot and making her the first casualty of the attack. But the gunshots alerted the security personnel in the premises, who moved fast to secure the building first, and thwart an attack on the heart of democracy.

Within no time a grenade exploded.

———

The Parliament House Building is a circular building with twelve entry points through huge wooden gates numbered one to twelve in the anticlockwise direction. Gate no. 11 is for the entry and exit of the vice president to the Parliament House and the other gates are used by different designated officials.

Around 11.20 a.m., the then vice president Krishan Kant had to leave for his residence. His carcade was stationed near gate no. 11. At about 11.35 a.m., the Ambassador car drove towards the carcade of the vice president. Since the escort vehicle, of which ASI Jeet Ram was in charge, was blocking the way, the car turned left. He called to stop the car, at which the driver reversed and, while doing so, struck the vice president's car. Jeet Ram and Shekher, the driver of the vice president's car, caught the collar of the driver of the car. The driver was manoeuvring the steering, which made Jeet Ram suspicious. He took out his revolver and fired at the driver, who was one of the terrorists. There was retaliatory firing in which Jeet Ram received a bullet injury to his right thigh.

The gunmen abandoned their car at gate no. 11 and ran towards gate no. 1. It was here that Head Constable Y.B. Thapa and Constable Sukhvinder Singh confronted them from behind a pillar. In the exchange of fire, a suicide bomber blew himself up.

The attackers were heavily armed with automatic assault rifles, pistols, and hand and rifle grenades. They were also carrying electronic detonators, spare ammunition and improvised explosive devices like tiffin bombs. In addition, the boot of the car contained a bomb made with an enormous quantity of ammonium nitrate. It was sufficient to blow up the entire Parliament premises.

At gate no. 9, D. Santosh Kumar, a young CRPF sepoy, positioned himself strategically behind a tree and shot three gunmen dead, thwarting their attempts to enter the Parliament.

'*Idhar se gher, udhar mar* [Encircle them from this side and hit that side]' was the command issued by Inspector Mohan Prasad, an elderly man on the verge of retirement. He guided his men throughout the attack, running from one gate to another. It was CRPF constable Shyambir Singh who finally killed the fifth terrorist.

The men in uniform killed with clinical precision. The gun battle lasted for about thirty minutes and all five intruders were killed.

Besides, nine people, including eight security personnel and one gardener, succumbed to bullets and sixteen people, including thirteen security men, received injuries. All the members of Parliament (MPs), including ministers, remained unhurt.

'I can never forget that day. I had come to Delhi from Assam only two months ago and was still getting a hang of Parliament security,' recalls Thapa, who was posted at gate no. 1 as guard commander, with Sukhvinder assisting him. The duo mistook the first grenade blast for a firecracker, but soon saw five men running and firing.

Thapa, who then limped to the CRPF tent even as bullets kept flying behind him, sustained bullet injuries to his leg. Sukhvinder too was shot in the abdomen, but survived.

Kamlesh Kumari was posthumously conferred with the Ashoka Chakra, the nation's highest peacetime award, by the then president of India, K.R. Narayanan, on Republic Day in 2002 as a tribute to 'her bravery and courage'. She is the second woman after Neerja Bhanot to have received this rare honour. Bhanot, a senior flight purser, was killed while saving passengers from heavily armed terrorists on-board the hijacked Pan Am Flight 73 at Karachi airport on 5 September 1986.

CRPF personnel Y.B. Thapa, D. Santosh Kumar, Sukhvinder Singh and Shyambir Singh were awarded the Shaurya Chakra and an out-of-turn promotion for exhibiting exemplary courage while countering and gunning down the terrorists.

The Parliament attack aroused both wrath and indignation. The then vice president Krishan Kant, the home minister L.K. Advani and the minister of state for defence Harin Pathak plus over a hundred people, including senior politicians, were still in the Parliament complex when the incident happened.

Police Action and the First Information Report

The police swung into action in no time. The station house officer (SHO) of the Parliament Street Police Station, G.L. Mehta, had the area cordoned off. The Bomb Disposal Squad of the National Security Guard (NSG) was called. A photographer and a crime team were also summoned to the spot.

The police seized various articles, including arms and ammunition, live and empty cartridges, and some incriminating documents. Blood samples and photographs of the five slain intruders were taken from various spots and the dead bodies were sent for post-mortem.

The SHO recorded the statement of S.I. Sham Singh, a prime witness who was in the vice president's security team. On the basis of this statement, a *rukka* (a document that records the occurrence of a bomb blast) was prepared. This formed the basis of the first information report (FIR). Further investigation was taken up by the special cell of the Delhi Police.

Investigations led to the seizure of the white Ambassador car. The home ministry sticker on the car was found to be fake. The car's rear windshield bore an inscription denigrating India and declaring a resolve to 'destroy' it. Six fake student identity cards were also recovered. The names on the identity cards—Anil Kumar, Raju Lal, Sunil Verma, Sanjay Koul, Rohail Sharma and Rohail Ali Shah—turned out to be aliases assumed by the gunmen.

Inspector Mohan Chand Sharma took over the investigations pertaining to phone call details and records.

The investigation narrowed down to three mobile numbers belonging to Mohammed Ajmal Amir Afzal (a political science graduate from the University of Delhi who was working as a commission agent/middleman in the fruits business when he was arrested), Syed Abdul Rehman Gilani (a lecturer of Arabic at Zakir Hussain College in the University of Delhi) and Shaukat Hussain Guru (a student of the University of Delhi).

Both Afzal and Shaukat were apprehended in a truck in Srinagar. The Srinagar Police arrested and brought them to Delhi in a special aircraft. A laptop and an amount of Rs 10 lakh were also recovered from the truck.

Disclosure Statement

On interrogation, Afzal and Shaukat not only made disclosures about their role in the conspiracy to attack the Parliament but also led the investigating team to various hideouts of the terrorists in Delhi. The investigations primarily led them to locations in Indira Vihar and Gandhi Vihar.

Afzal identified the bodies of the five slain men at the Lady Hardinge Medical College Hospital. He also led the Delhi Police to the shops from where the chemicals required for preparing explosives and other materials such as the red beacon were acquired. The other items traced to the terrorists included a motorcycle, dry fruit, mobile phones, etc.

The forensic analysis revealed the documents found at the spot with the slain gunmen—including the fake identity cards and the sticker of the home ministry—were stored in their laptop in electronic form.

Rajbir Singh, ACP, Special Cell, took over the investigation of the attack on 19 December 2001. On this day, evidence was also collected by police through the interception of communications between the accused and others under the stringent provisions of the Prevention of Terrorism Act (POTA). This subsequent invocation of POTA was contested vehemently by the accused in all three courts. They claimed that it was unjustified to invoke it when the investigating officer had not done so on the very first day when the FIR was registered. Singh interrogated Afzal the next day and recorded his supplementary disclosure statement. The three accused, Afzal, Shaukat and Gilani, expressed their desire to make confessional statements before the deputy commissioner of police (DCP).

Afzal was produced before Ashok Chand, DCP, Special Cell, and the record has it that Chand asked the ACP to leave the room. The DCP explained to Afzal that he was not bound to make the confessional statement and if he did it could be used against him as evidence. The court documents reveal that Afzal was not under any duress and his signature was recorded beneath his endorsement. Afzal and the other two accused were later produced before the Additional Chief Metropolitan Magistrate (ACMM) of Patiala House Court, V.K. Maheshwari, on 22 December 2001 for recording their statements. Afzal and Shaukat later confirmed having made the confessional statements without any threat or pressure and signed the statements acknowledging the confession made to the DCP.

In legal parlance, confessions are considered highly reliable because it is presumed that no rational person would make an admission against his interest unless prompted by his conscience to tell the truth.

The confession detailed Afzal joining the Jammu Kashmir Liberation Front (JKLF), a militant outfit, in 1989–90. He mentioned that he was trained in insurgent activities in Pakistan-Occupied Kashmir (PoK) after which he returned to India.

> I came to Delhi with my cousin Shaukat for studies. Here, I met Gilani while studying in the Delhi University . . . In 1993, I surrendered before the BSF [Border Security Force] on the advice of my family members. I returned to my native place Sopore and started a commission agency business. It was during this time that I came into contact with Tariq from Anantnag [in Kashmir]. It's Tariq who motivated me to join jihad for the liberation of Kashmir.

Tariq also introduced Afzal to Ghazi Baba, a Jaish-e-Mohammad (JeM) leader in Kashmir, and the prime accused in the attack. 'It was Ghazi Baba who exhorted me to join the movement and to carry out attacks on important institutions in India like the Parliament and embassies and asked me to find a safe hideout for the fidayeens in Delhi. During that meeting, I was introduced to Mohammed and Haider, Pakistani nationals and militants,' he told the police.

Afzal had come to Delhi with Mohammed in the first week of November. Mohammed bought a laptop for Afzal and collected money through hawala. Shaukat, who was Afzal's cousin, arranged for safe hideouts. Tariq sent these militants, who were carrying rifles with loaded magazines, grenade launchers, pistols, hand grenades and shells, electric detonators and other explosives, to Delhi.

'We purchased ammonium nitrate, aluminium powder, sulphur and other items to prepare bombs and explosives to help carry out the task assigned by Ghazi Baba,' Afzal confessed.

Mohammed purchased mobile phones and SIM cards and received directions from Ghazi Baba via a satellite phone. It was Mohammed who suggested to Ghazi Baba that they target the Parliament. A meeting was held in Shaukat's house and plans for the attack were finalized.

'As per the plan, we bought a second-hand Ambassador car from Karol Bagh on December 11. We also purchased a magnetic VIP red light,' he said. While Mohammed prepared a fake sticker of the Ministry of Home Affairs and identity cards using his laptop, Afzal and other militants prepared improvised explosive devices (IEDs), one of which was fitted in the white Ambassador.

Afzal, along with co-accused Shaukat and Gilani, visited the five Pakistani terrorists at their hideouts in Gandhi Vihar on the night of 12 December. Mohammed gave Afzal Rs 10 lakh meant for him, Shaukat and Gilani. He also gave them the laptop, which was to be delivered to Ghazi Baba.

Mohammed told them that they had to conduct a fidayeen attack on the Parliament House on 31 December 2001.

'And then I left for Kashmir with Shaukat in his truck, but we were apprehended by the J&K police on December 15 and brought to Delhi. The police also recovered the laptop and the accessories and Rs 10 lakh,' said Mohammed, as noted by the ACMM.

According to the confession, Afzal and Mohammed had remained in touch and on 13 December Afzal had received a call from Mohammed asking him to watch TV and inform him about the presence of VVIPs at the Parliament House.

The Trial

Delhi Police filed the report under Section 173 of the Code of Criminal Procedure (CrPC) against the four accused, including Shaukat's wife, Afsan Guru. Afsan (formerly Navjot Sandhu) was a Sikh girl, who converted to Islam at the time of marriage. Gilani had played a part in their marriage ceremony in 2000.

Charges were framed on 14 May 2002 under various sections of the Indian Penal Code (IPC), POTA, 2002, and the Explosive Substances Act by the designated special court presided over by S.N. Dhingra.

The charges included waging or attempting to wage war against the government of India and the conspiracy to commit the same; collecting arms, etc., with the intention of waging war against the government; criminal conspiracy to commit murder; conspiracy to commit a terrorist act; voluntarily harbouring a terrorist, etc.

Ninety witnesses were examined and about 330 documents were relied upon in support of the charges against the accused. When Afzal declined to engage a counsel on his own, the trial judge took measures to provide effective legal aid to him and appointed lawyer Seema Gulati and her junior Neeraj Bansal to defend him. When his counsel conceded that there was, prima facie, sufficient material to frame charges, the court did so against all the accused on 4 June 2002. The accused pleaded not guilty. Next day, all the counsel appearing for the accused agreed that post-mortem reports, medico-legal cases, documents related to the recovery of guns and explosive substances at the crime spot should be considered undisputed evidence without formal proof. This resulted in the dropping of a considerable number of witnesses for the prosecution.

On 1 July, Gulati sought discharge from the case as Afzal said that she neither took instructions from him nor discussed the case with him. Since the judge was not satisfied with the plea, Bansal, who had filed a *vakalatnama* (a document signed by an accused and others giving authority to an advocate to plead and argue his or her case), along with Gulati earlier, was then nominated as the amicus curiae to defend Afzal. No objection was raised by Afzal then. It was only later, on 8 July, that Afzal filed an application stating that he was not satisfied with Bansal and needed a senior lawyer to defend him. On 12 July, the trial judge recorded that the four counsel named by Afzal were not willing to take up his case and, therefore, Bansal continued. Afzal was given the opportunity to cross-examine the prosecution witnesses in addition to the amicus curiae.

During the hearing, the trial court had declared as valid the evidence collected by the police through the interception of communications under the provisions of POTA. Dhingra in his order had recorded that the '[e]vidence collected by various police officials when the case was registered under different provisions of the law i.e. Indian Penal Code, Explosives Substance Act and Arms Act cannot be washed out merely because on December 19, 2001, provisions of POTA were not part of the FIR and investigation.'

'The evidence collected by the police between December 13 and 19 cannot be eschewed and the investigation in this regard cannot be said to be null and void,' the designated judge S.N. Dhingra had said while dismissing the applications of the three accused persons, including a JeM militant seeking the exclusion of evidence obtained through interception of communication. The three accused—Afzal, Shaukat and Gilani—were each convicted of the offences and awarded the death penalty by the designated judge on 18 December 2002. Additionally, Shaukat's wife, Afsan, was sentenced to a rigorous imprisonment of five years and fined Rs 10,000 for the less serious charge of concealing the knowledge of the conspiracy.

When the judge left the courtroom after pronouncing the sentence, lawyers at the Patiala House Courts started to shout, 'Kill them, they are terrorists.' As information about the ruling spread, people burst crackers outside the court.

Upset with the trial court's order, all the three convicts moved the Delhi High Court, which confirmed the death sentence for Afzal and Shaukat on 29 October 2003. The Division Bench comprising justices Usha Mehra and Pradeep Nandrajog, in a 392-page judgment, held that 'the offence is of a magnitude that the collective conscious of the community is so shocked that it will expect the holders of the judicial power centre to inflict death penalty irrespective of their personal opinion as regards desirability or otherwise of retaining the death penalty.'

However, the HC judges acquitted Gilani on the grounds that there was no conclusive evidence against him.

We are left with only one piece of evidence against him—the record of telephone calls between him and Afzal and Shaukat. This circumstance . . . does not even remotely, far less definitely and unerringly, point towards the guilt of Gilani. We, therefore, conclude that the prosecution has failed to bring on record evidence, which cumulatively forms a chain, so complete that there is no escape from the conclusion that in all human probabilities Gilani was involved in the conspiracy.

Afsan was also acquitted as the judges held that the 'scanty evidence' did not prove that she had knowledge of the plan to attack the Parliament before it happened.

The Supreme Court's Judgment

On seven cross-appeals—four by the National Capital Territory of Delhi against the acquittal of Gilani and Afsan, one by Afzal and two by Shaukat—the Supreme Court on 4 August 2005 confirmed the death sentence for Afzal. They further sentenced Shaukat to ten years of rigorous imprisonment, saying there was clinching evidence against Afzal regarding his nexus with the terrorists who carried out the 'terrorist act of the most diabolical nature'.

There was not even a shred of doubt about his complicity in hatching the criminal conspiracy to attack the Parliament and evidence showed that he had actively participated in its execution, the bench said. 'All evidences unerringly point to Afzal, a key conspirator, who played an active role,' the bench comprising justices P.V. Reddi and P.P. Naolekar said, while observing that by no standards could his act be termed 'innocuous'.

Afzal was also given the life sentence on three counts, but as he was sentenced to death, the sentence of life imprisonment was naturally merged with the death sentence.

Although the apex court affirmed the acquittal of Gilani, it pointed the needle of suspicion at him. The apex court said that Gilani's conduct raised a 'serious suspicion that he was approving of the happenings in Delhi'—he had rejoiced and 'laughed heartily when the Delhi event was raised in [a] conversation with his cousin'.

Even the 'untruthful pleas raised by him about his contact with Shaukat and Afzal give rise to serious suspicion at least about his knowledge of the incident and his tacit approval of it,' the apex court said. However, it added, 'At the same time, suspicion, however strong, cannot take the place of legal proof. Though his conduct was not above board, the court cannot condemn him in the absence of sufficient evidence pointing unmistakably to his guilt.'

The top court had noted that he was on intimate terms with Shaukat and Afzal, was conversing with them frequently and that there were 'contemporaneous' calls between them as well. However, the calls did not hold as definite pointers to Gilani's involvement in the conspiracy to attack the Parliament.

The Supreme Court, in its 107-page judgment, observed:

There can be no doubt that the most appropriate punishment is death sentence . . . the present case, which has no parallel in the history of Indian Republic, presents us in crystal clear terms, a spectacle of rarest of rare cases. The very idea of attacking and overpowering a sovereign democratic institution by using powerful arms and explosives and imperilling the safety of a multitude of peoples' representatives, constitutional functionaries and officials of the government of India and engaging in a combat with security forces is a terrorist act of gravest severity.

The judgment further stated:

The incident . . . had shaken the entire nation and the collective conscience of the society will only be satisfied if the capital punishment is awarded to the offender. The challenge to the unity, integrity and sovereignty of India by these acts of terrorists and conspirators, can only be compensated by giving the maximum punishment to the person who is proved to be the conspirator in this treacherous act. The appellant (Afzal), who is a surrendered militant and who was bent upon repeating the acts of treason against the nation, is a menace to the society and his life should become extinct. Accordingly, we uphold the death sentence.

Considering Afzal's confessional statement to the Delhi Police Special Cell, the top court concluded that the circumstances clearly established Afzal's association with the terrorists 'in almost every act done by them in order to achieve the objective of attacking the Parliament House'. 'Short of participating in the actual attack,' Afzal, the apex court said, 'did everything to set in motion the diabolical mission'.

The court held that Afzal had been a part of the nexus

between the conspirators and terrorists and was involved in almost every task that brought about the attack on the Parliament. Not only was he a party to the conspiracy but had also played an active part in its furtherance.

These circumstances could not be viewed in isolation and 'by no standards of common sense, be regarded as innocuous acts. His conduct and actions—antecedent, contemporaneous and subsequent—all point to his guilt,' the apex court said.

The adherence to and violation of procedures during the trial were argued at length by the lawyers of the accused. Various technical issues were also raised. Veteran criminal lawyer Ram Jethmalani, who appeared for Gilani, contended that the Lt Governor of the National Capital Territory of Delhi was not competent to give sanctions under POTA and only the Central government could have done so. He cited two provisions to prove his point, stressing that under both Section 50 of POTA and Section 196 of the IPC, the court can take cognizance of offences only after the prior approval of the Central government or the state government. However, the argument was rejected by the apex court, which held that the sanction accorded by the Lt Governor in this case was a valid sanction under both the laws.

The Supreme Court did not find fault with the investigating officers for failing to bring POTA into the picture sooner. 'At any rate, it may be a case of bona fide error or overcautious approach,' stated the court by way of explanation. Various technicalities were also pointed out by Afzal's lawyers but failed to satisfy the judges. Senior counsel Sushil Kumar pointed out that the lawyer appointed by the trial court as amicus curiae to take care of his client's (Afzal's) defence was thrust upon him against his will. However, the Supreme Court rejected the stand and ruled out the claim that Afzal had been denied the facility of effective defence.

Senior counsel Gopal Subramanium, appearing for the state, rubbished Kumar's contentions that improper confessional procedures had been carried out by the police; he reiterated that the confessional statement of Afzal was already recorded by the DCP, who had done so only after issuing adequate statutory warning. He also asserted that this had been done at a place away from the police station, and that Afzal was given time for reflection. The confession was recorded only after making sure that Afzal was volunteering to make the confession in an atmosphere free from threat or inducement. 'There was perfect compliance,' Subramanium stressed.

The state counsel said that Afzal was even produced before the ACMM on the very next day, 22 December 2001, along with the confessional statements, which were kept in a sealed cover. The ACMM opened the cover, perused the confessional statements, called Afzal into his chamber and made it known to him that he was not legally bound to make the confession. It was only after Afzal indicated that he understood his position that he voluntarily made the confession without any threat or coercion—this was recorded by the ACMM in the statement, Subramanium added. He also mentioned that no traces of any physical violence were found on Afzal and the other accused during the medical examination.

Soon the counsel for the accused fired another salvo. He claimed that sufficient time was not given to Afzal and Shaukat for reflection after they were produced for the recording of the confession. They were given only five to ten minutes to think and reflect, which, by all standards, was inadequate, Afzal's lawyer argued.

Granting reasonable time for reflection before recording a confession is one way of ensuring that the person concerned gets the opportunity to deliberate and introspect once again.

However, all the arguments were strongly challenged by Subramanium. He contended that there was no hard and fast rule regarding the grant of time for reflection and the rules and guidelines applicable to a confession under Section 164 of the CrPC don't govern the case. Besides, Subramanium emphasized that Afzal did not lodge any protest or complaint but reaffirmed the factum of making his confession when Shaukat and he were produced before the ACMM the day after the POTA charges were added.

POTA, which the Atal Bihari Vajpayee–led National Democratic Alliance government had introduced in June 2002 to deal with terrorist activities in India, was repealed by its successor, the United Progressive Alliance, in September 2004. The abolition of POTA was the Manmohan Singh government's first major policy decision after taking office in May 2004. POTA had replaced the Terrorist and Disruptive Activities (Prevention) Act (TADA), which was allowed to lapse by the P.V. Narasimha Rao government back in 1995. POTA allowed the detention of a suspect for up to 180 days without the filing of charges in court. It also allowed law enforcement agencies to treat a confession made to the police as an admission of guilt, which is not the case under other related laws. A person can deny such confessions in court, but not under POTA.

It was advocate Kamini Jaiswal who had fought with Jethmalani to defend Gilani in the case. During one of the hearings in another case in the apex court, the noted criminal lawyer and former law minister Jethmalani had conceded that defending Gilani had almost cost him his political career. 'I appeared for the man in both the high court and the Supreme Court and was almost thrown out of politics. The question posed to me was—how could I appear for a man sentenced to death in the case relating to terror attack on the Parliament, the symbol of India's sovereignty? But to the credit of the HC and the SC, both saw that there was no weight in the evidence presented against Gilani,' he had argued.[1] In order to be assured of the truth of the confession, the Supreme Court, in a series of decisions, has evolved a rule of prudence that prescribes that the court should look to corroborate the confession against other evidence. Broadly, there should be corroboration so that the confession taken as a whole fits into the facts proved by other evidence.

Later in 2007, the Supreme Court dismissed Afzal's plea seeking a review of his death sentence for the lack of merit in it.

The verdict evoked varied reactions from different quarters. Some academicians, social activists and lawyers raised issues after the judicial process was over. A few demanded a reinvestigation into the case and wanted the President to commute Afzal's death sentence as he had already served more than a decade in prison.

However, many felt that reopening the case was not required since the criticism and debate after the hanging of Afzal concerned the role of the judiciary and the executive.

According to journalist-turned-lawyer Gyanant Singh, who covered the case as a journalist:

> This was not an in-camera trial. There was no veil of secrecy. The process of trial and the appeals gave opportunities for raising all defences. In fact, the issue of procedural lapses was raised and the debate concluded with the finding of the court. Such debates on merits of evidence at a subsequent stage are counter-productive and cannot take place without questioning the very foundation of the justice delivery system.

The media also reported that separatist groups such as JKLF and Hurriyat factions were threatening to turn the hanging into an issue. JKLF supremo Yasin Malik, too, warned of disastrous consequences if Afzal was hanged.

While there was resentment against the execution verdict, the family of deceased constable Kamlesh Kumari (the slain CRPF constable) announced: 'We would return the Ashoka Chakra if the President heeds to the mercy plea.'

It was in February 2013 that President Pranab Mukherjee rejected Afzal's mercy petition. Afzal was hanged on 9 February 2013 in Delhi's Tihar Jail.

His hanging, dubbed Operation Three Star, was kept an ultra-secret affair in order to avert any repercussions in his home state of Jammu and Kashmir. His family was allegedly not informed prior to his execution and his dead body was not given to them for fears that his funeral could have become an 'occasion for a demonstration' by separatists and vested interests.

The decision to bury Afzal inside Tihar's jail no. 3 in the maximum-security prison complex was made to prevent Jammu and Kashmir's pro-Pakistan secessionists from deriving political mileage from his grave.[2] Similar precautions had been taken in the case of Kashmiri terrorist Maqbool Butt who was hanged in 1984.

However, the then Union home minister Sushil Kumar Shinde rejected the allegations of not having informed Afzal's family before his hanging. He said that Afzal's family was informed on time, but the speed-post letter sent by the jail authorities reached his family two days after his hanging. The hanging wouldn't have been possible if the decision had been made public in advance, he had said while defending the secrecy enshrouding Afzal's execution.

When Afzal was told about his execution, he had expressed his wish to write to his wife. He wrote a letter in Urdu, which was delivered to his family on 12 February. The letter, which he wrote at 6.25 a.m., just one hour and thirty-five minutes before his hanging, expressed his gratitude to God for choosing him for all that he had done. He, however, had no personal message for his wife or his son.

On the day of his hanging, he savoured a cup of tea. In fact, he requested for another cup and hummed a popular Bollywood song *Apne liye jiye toh kya jiye, tu jee ae dil zamane ke liye* (If you live for yourself, what's the use? You must live for the world). He would often sing this song, apart from socializing and playing badminton. The jail authorities said he often read books as well. He remained sober all through and did not betray any sign of repentance.

Legal experts flayed the government over the manner of

execution. They felt that the executive could have handled the situation better by allowing a secret meeting with Afzal's family. 'As regards denying the right over dead body and burial, this was not done for the first time. Assassins of Prime Minister Indira Gandhi were also cremated in jail,' said Gyanant Singh.

Reactions

Afzal's execution elicited varying reactions. The hanging was ordered less than three months after Mohammed Ajmal Amir Kasab, the lone surviving terrorist convicted in the 2008 Mumbai attacks case, was executed. There was speculation that the government would move quickly to execute him as many political parties had mounted pressure for Afzal's immediate execution.

In fact, one of the election slogans of the Bharatiya Janata Party (BJP) was '*Desh abhi sharminda hai, Afzal abhibhi zinda hai* [The country is ashamed as Afzal is still alive].'

Most political parties, with the exception of the ones from Kashmir, hailed the move to execute Afzal. The Congress party, the BJP and the Communist Party of India (Marxist) or CPI (M) were united in hailing the apex court judgment as the triumph of the rule of law.

'I think, the law of the land, with all its provisions, has finally been completed in the case. The issue had been lingering for the past 11 years and has finally completed its due course,' said CPI (M) Politburo member Sitaram Yechury.[3]

Narendra Modi, as the then chief minister of Gujarat, had

tweeted 'Better late than never' after the news of the hanging was announced.

Justice S.N. Dhingra, who had ordered the gallows for Afzal in 2002, praised the execution, saying, 'Finally, justice has been delivered.' Criticizing the President for the delay, he said that the judiciary had swiftly concluded the trial within six months, but Afzal's mercy petition lay pending with the President's office for almost seven years. 'It reflects the casual approach of the government to curb terrorism,' he observed. He also took a dig at the government, saying that 'the secret execution shows fear psychosis'.[4]

But unlike Kasab's execution, which sparked celebrations all over the country, Afzal's case was seen as more divisive. His execution resulted in violent protests across Kashmir.

The All Parties Hurriyat Conference (APHC), a separatist organization, announced a four-day mourning on Afzal's death. Hurriyat chairman Syed Ali Shah Geelani called Afzal 'an icon of the Kashmiri resistance'. Hilal Ahmad War, a leader of a separatist faction, said that 'the hanging of Afzal is a declaration of war by India'.[5] Kashmiri Muslim separatist leaders warned that his hanging would fuel the revolt in Kashmir, where security forces have been battling terrorism for about three decades.

Several leaders of the separatist movement were also detained to maintain peace. Even co-accused Syed Abdul Rehman Gilani was taken into preventive custody by the Delhi Police.

The police enforced prohibitory orders and curfew was imposed in the Valley to prevent any kind of protests in support of Afzal. Cable TV and Internet services were shut down to stop separatists from organizing and spreading unrest. Mosques were used for public announcements and curfew information.

The Central government did follow the advice issued by the Jammu and Kashmir government—to carry out the execution only on a weekend in order to eliminate the possibility of secessionists using Friday prayers to whip up passions. The prudence did work to a large extent.

However, protests still flared up in parts of the Valley and most of the violence was reported from Afzal's home district Sopore, Baramulla, in north Kashmir. Thirty-six people including twenty-three policemen were injured in protests. Scuffles also broke out in New Delhi.

Even though he was critical of Afzal's 'out-of-turn' hanging, the then chief minister of Jammu and Kashmir Omar Abdullah also made a televised appeal for calm. He commented that the 'biggest tragedy' of the execution was that Afzal was not allowed to meet his family before being hanged. He also accused the Centre of being 'selective' in avenging attacks on the symbols of democracy and backed the allegation that the legal process in Afzal's case was 'flawed'. State officials praised the army and security forces for their measured response.

Not surprisingly, some social and legal activists have issues with capital punishment in principle, its award to Afzal and the manner of his execution. Calling the hanging an 'irresponsible, careless and inhuman act', Kamini Jaiswal criticized the government for maintaining such secrecy that Afzal's wife was also not informed about her husband's hanging.

Ram Jethmalani said that life imprisonment for Afzal

should have been all right as he was only accompanying those who attacked the Parliament. 'Life imprisonment is bigger than any doctrine that you will go to heaven (after getting death punishment). You must keep him in jail for life.'

Afzal's hanging also revived the ongoing debate on capital punishment and brought to the forefront the trail that accompanies every trial—the issue of fairness, legal representation and other technical nuances.

Nandita Haksar, who had campaigned for Afzal, wrote in her column on *Mainstream Weekly* that he did not get a fair trial and had no chance to represent himself as 'he was too poor to pay the fees for a lawyer, and even those who he named refused to represent him (including a well-known human rights lawyer). The lawyer foisted on him by the Sessions Judge did not want to represent Afzal.'[6]

Human rights body Amnesty International said that Afzal's execution indicated a 'disturbing and regressive trend towards execution shrouded in secrecy and the resumption of death penalty use in India'. It also opposed the death penalty in all circumstances as an inherently irreversible, inhumane punishment. Others saw it as a distressing step after an eight-year moratorium on the death penalty.

A War against the Government of India

The single most important factor pointed out by the Supreme Court was that Afzal had conspired to wage war against the nation and the support he extended to carry out the criminal conspiracy made him a 'menace to society'. The Supreme Court bench wrote in its judgment:

The target chosen was Parliament, a symbol of sovereignty of the Indian republic. Comprised of peoples' representatives, this supreme law-making body steers the destinies of vast multitude of Indian people. It is a constitutional repository of sovereign power that collectively belongs to the people of India . . . the attempted attack on Parliament is an undoubted invasion of the sovereign attribute of the State, including the government of India, which is its alter ego. The attack of this nature cannot be viewed on the same footing as a terrorist attack on some public office building or an incident resulting in the breach of public tranquility.

According to the Supreme Court judgment, Afzal's case did injure the collective conscience of our society and only capital punishment could have brought about the proper purgation of enraged sentiments. His death sentence was a step forward to regain and strengthen our social solidarity. The general sentiment of the court was:

The unity, integrity and sovereignty of India is an expression of collective conscience of each citizen, their beliefs, ideas, attitudes, and knowledge that are common to our society. It is this sense of collective consciousness that informs our sense of belongingness and identity, and our behaviour. The incident, which resulted in heavy casualties, had shaken the entire nation and the collective conscience of the society will only be satisfied if the capital punishment is awarded to the offender.

The attack on the Parliament has no parallel in the history

of the Indian Republic and is a classic example of the rarest of rare cases. The court said:

> The very idea of attacking and overpowering a sovereign democratic institution by using powerful arms and explosives and imperiling the safety of a multitude of peoples' representatives, constitutional functionaries and officials of the Government of India and engaging into a combat with security forces is a terrorist act of the gravest severity.

The death penalty jurisprudence has been widely debated in India. The Supreme Court had earlier advocated the three-test theory in deciding death-penalty cases. The three tests have to be satisfied before awarding the death penalty.

> The crime test, meaning the aggravating circumstances of the case; the criminal test, meaning that there should be no mitigating circumstance favouring the accused; and if both tests are satisfied, then the rarest of rare cases test, which depends on the perception of society and not 'judge-centric', that is whether society will approve of the awarding of death sentence in certain types of crime or not. While applying this test, the court has to look into a variety of factors, such as society's abhorrence, extreme indignation and antipathy to certain types of crimes.[7]

However, Amnesty International India and the People's Union for Civil Liberties (PUCL) research into Supreme Court judgments on the death penalty terms the capital punishment a 'lethal lottery' and 'highly arbitrary'.[8] Amnesty International India has claimed that 'the administration of the death penalty, in practice, is affected by several factors, ranging from the competence of legal representation to the personal views of judges'.

However, the Law Commission of India, which suggests legal reforms to the government, in its recommendations in 2015 favoured the abolition of the death penalty, except in cases of terror and waging war against the state.

The panel, in its 262nd report on the issue of the death penalty in India, discussed a wide range of issues from death penalty not being a deterrent to changing international and national scenarios to arbitrariness in decision-making and the existence of bias as some of the reasons for recommending the abolition of the death penalty, except in the case of terrorism-related offences.

The commission concluded that the death penalty does not serve the goal of deterrence any more than life imprisonment does. It also recommended various provisions for police reforms, schemes for witness protection and victim compensation. The commission felt that the time has come for India to move towards the abolition of the death penalty.

Further, the collective conscience of people who do not support capital punishment is gradually gaining momentum in India, although they are still perceived to be a minority. They feel that the death penalty creates no deterrence, and that life imprisonment is an equally rigorous punishment.

2

Nirbhaya

The Case That Shook the Nation

'There are things of which I may not speak;
There are dreams that cannot die;
There are thoughts that make the strong heart weak,
And bring a pallor into the cheek,
And a mist before the eye.'

—Henry Wadsworth Longfellow

The story of Nirbhaya can only moisten your eyes. The year 2012 ended on a sad note for India. A hair-raising and spine-chilling incident left the country in a state of shock. Twenty-three-year-old Nirbhaya (name given by the media), a physiotherapy student, was gang-raped in a moving bus in south Delhi. The gory tragedy lasted for more than an hour before she was thrown out of the bus and left severely injured on the side of the road near Mahipalpur flyover on National Highway 8. The physiotherapy student had gone to watch a film with her friend Awindra Pratap Pandey at PVR Select

City Mall, Saket, on 16 December 2012. They were returning home and boarded an off-duty charter bus at Munirka on Sunday at about 9.30 p.m.

On that fateful night, the private bus began moving at a reasonable speed, after which the lights were switched off. A few minutes later three people, including a juvenile, emerged from the driver's cabin. Nirbhaya and Awindra sat huddled together, snuggling not to escape the cold but the looming fear. Panic and fear began to grip them. Armed with iron rods, the men provoked and abused Awindra, an altercation followed and two more people joined them.

Awindra was thrashed and severely beaten up with iron rods during those eighty-four minutes of horror. The rods caused injuries to his head, legs and other parts of the body, leaving him in a semi-conscious state. They also snatched his belongings—mobile phone, watch, rings, debit and credit cards—and removed his clothes and shoes.

Nirbhaya was dragged to the rear of the bus. She kept on yelling '*Bachao, bachao* [Save me, save me]'. Her screams went unheard and unanswered.

She was brutally gang-raped and also subjected to unnatural sex. Her private parts and internal organs were ruptured by inserting iron rods and hands. Awindra could hear her painful cries, but he lay hapless and helpless. The ordeal didn't end here. The accused kept saying that they should not be kept alive.

Nirbhaya and Awindra were thrown out of the moving bus near the Mahipalpur flyover, by the side of the road. While the semi-clad Awindra shouted for help, Nirbhaya was lying naked in a pool of blood. As they lay on the road, their tormentors tried to silence them by running the bus over them and finally left them for dead.

Raj Kumar, a patrolman who heard the distress calls, informed the police and organized the Police Control Room van. At about 10.24 p.m., Head Constable Ram Chander, after receiving the information, reached the site and dispersed the crowd. He brought some water and a bed sheet from a nearby hotel, and tore it into two parts to cover the victims. He then rushed them to the Safdarjung Hospital. Awindra was examined in the casualty and Nirbhaya was admitted in the gynaecology ward. It was here that she shared her trauma with Dr Rashmi Ahuja: 'I was slapped, kicked on my abdomen and bitten over lips, cheeks, breasts and in the vulval region.' She narrated how she had resisted unnatural oral sex and how she was dragged and thrown out of the bus.

At about 3.45 a.m. on 17 December 2012, Awindra Pratap gave his statement to the Delhi Police, which culminated in the recording of an FIR at 5.40 a.m. at the Vasant Vihar Police Station. While Awindra was narrating his statement to the police, Nirbhaya underwent her first surgery at 4 a.m. The second and third surgeries were performed on 19 and 23 December, respectively.

With the help of highway CCTV, the bus was traced and its driver Ram Singh arrested. Singh's disclosure statement led to the discovery of his bloodstained clothes, iron rods and the debit card of Asha Devi, Nirbhaya's mother. Singh's arrest led the police to Vinay Sharma and Pawan Gupta. The next day, Mukesh Singh was apprehended from a village called Karoli. In a Test Identification Parade (TIP), Awindra identified accused Mukesh Singh. Soon after, Akshay Thakur was nabbed from Aurangabad, Bihar. Raju, a seventeen-year-old juvenile, too was arrested.

The news of such a gory incident in the capital city enraged people. Thousands protested at India Gate and Raisina Hill on 21 December. They clashed with the police and the Rapid Action Force (RAF). The police had to resort to lathi charge and deter them with water cannons and tear-gas shells. They were also baton-charged and some were arrested.

Similar protests took place throughout the country. Protests occurred on the social networking sites Facebook and WhatsApp too, with users replacing their profile pictures with a black dot. A black dot was publicly used to symbolize shame and as an image of pain, injustice, anger and helplessness. Online petitions were signed to demand justice in the case. Silent and candlelight marches were taken out. Protesters also formed human chains at various places and took a vow 'to respect girls' and seek 'justice for Nirbhaya'.

Yoga guru Baba Ramdev and former army chief general Vijay Kumar Singh too were a part of these protests at Jantar Mantar. With the protestors swelling in the capital, the police closed down seven metro stations and restricted the roads leading to India Gate. Curfew was imposed around Rashtrapati Bhavan along with Section 144 of the CrPC to avoid large gatherings of people at Raisina Hill.

On 21 December, the government appointed a committee of physicians to ensure that Nirbhaya received the best medical care. The then chief minister of Delhi, Sheila Dikshit, took the decision to fly her to Singapore's Mount Elizabeth Hospital, a multi-organ transplant specialty hospital. On 27 December, during a six-hour flight in an air ambulance, Nirbhaya suffered a cardiac arrest. The doctors on board created an arterial line to stabilize her, but she had been without pulse and blood pressure for nearly three minutes and never regained consciousness after that. Her condition deteriorated further and she died at 2.15 a.m. on 29 December in Singapore. The cause of her death was sepsis with multiple organ failure following multiple injuries. Her body was flown back in a special Air India aircraft and she was cremated on 30 December in Delhi under high police security. Fearing law-and-order problems, the government ensured that Nirbhaya's cremation plans were kept a secret.

Prime Minister Manmohan Singh and Congress President Sonia Gandhi went to the airport to receive the body and console the family. A large number of Delhi Police, RAF and Border Security Force (BSF) personnel in riot gear accompanied the ambulance carrying the body to her house before the cremation.

The authorities wanted the last rites to be performed at 6.30 a.m. but Hindu traditions did not allow cremation before sunrise. At 7.30 a.m., Nirbhaya's father lit the funeral pyre in the presence of her brothers, relatives and others.

Many dignitaries including the then chief minister Sheila Dikshit, the minister of state for the home ministry R.P.N. Singh, west Delhi MP Mahabal Mishra and Delhi BJP chief Vijender Gupta attended the cremation.

Dying Declaration

Before Nirbhaya was flown to Singapore, she issued three recorded dying declarations—the last of which was expressed in gestures. The police maintained that all three declarations were recorded at the victim's instance, a fact that was corroborated by medical evidence. Subdivisional Magistrate Usha Chaturvedi and Metropolitan Magistrate Pawan Kumar recorded her statements one after the other. On 25 December, Kumar recorded the final dying declaration at 1 p.m. Nirbhaya was not in a position to speak but was conscious and responded by way of gestures. In a sensitive way, the magistrate carried out the operation using multiple-choice questions.

A dying declaration is recorded as it can provide the sole basis of conviction if it inspires the full confidence of the court and is free from infirmities. The court is supposed to examine the contents of the dying declaration in the light of the various surrounding facts and circumstances. The one made by Nirbhaya was corroborated with oral and documentary evidence and also with medical evidence.

Awindra Pratap Pandey, Nirbhaya's friend, testified in the trial court on 19 December 2012. He recorded his statement with a subdivisional magistrate at the Safdarjung Hospital and later on 21 December in the presence of the Deputy Commissioner of Police.

Following public outrage and demands for a speedy trial and prosecution, the police promised to file the charge sheet within one week. The Parliamentary Standing Committee on Home Affairs met on 27 December to discuss the issue, and Union Home Secretary R.K. Singh and Delhi Police Commissioner Neeraj Kumar were summoned to appear.

The Delhi High Court approved the creation of five fast-track courts to try rape and sexual assault cases. The first of the five approved fast-track courts was inaugurated on 2 January 2013 by the late chief justice of India Altamas Kabir in the Saket Court Complex of south Delhi.

The Juvenile Justice Board (JJB) declared Mohammad Afroz alias Raju to be seventeen years and six months old and rejected the police request for a bone-ossification test for a positive documentation of his age. The minor, since established as the 'most brutal' of the six accused, was tried separately in a juvenile court. On 31 August, he was convicted of rape and murder under the Juvenile Justice Act and given the maximum sentence of three years' imprisonment in a reform facility, inclusive of the eight months he had spent in remand during the trial. The juvenile was released on 20 December 2015.

Five days after Nirbhaya's death, on 3 January 2013, the police filed the charge sheet against the six men for rape, murder, kidnapping, destruction of evidence and the attempted murder of Awindra. Senior lawyer Dayan Krishnan was appointed as the special public prosecutor. During the trial, the prime accused Ram Singh committed suicide by hanging himself in Tihar jail. The other four accused— Mukesh Singh, Vinay Sharma, Akshay Thakur and Pawan Gupta—denied charges. Some of the men had confessed earlier to the crime, however their lawyers later denied their confession. They said that their clients were tortured to admit the crime and that their confessions had been coerced.

On 10 September 2013, sessions judge Yogesh Khanna convicted all the four accused persons and awarded them the death penalty under Section 120(B) of the IPC for the offence of criminal conspiracy, and also for abducting the victims with an intention to force illicit intercourse and for attempting to kill.

Rejecting the pleas for a lesser sentence, the judge said that the case had 'shocked the collective conscience of India' and that 'courts cannot turn a blind eye to such crimes'.

'We were waiting with bated breath, now we are relieved. I thank the people of my country and the media,' said Nirbhaya's mother.[1]

Six months thereafter, on 13 March 2014, the Delhi High Court upheld their conviction and sentence. The court noted that the crime, which stirred widespread protests over sexual crimes against women in the country, fell into the judicial system's 'rarest of rare' category, which allows capital punishment.

All the convicts then approached the Supreme Court, which in 2014 stayed their execution.

On 5 May 2017, a three-judge bench of the Supreme Court upheld the death sentence of the four convicts in the 2012 Delhi gang-rape and murder case, which had shaken the entire nation with its brutality.

'She was an object for their enjoyment . . . for their gross, sadistic pleasures . . . for the devilish manner in which they played with her dignity and identity.' These were the final words with which Justice Dipak Misra pronounced the judgment confirming the death penalty.

Highlighting the extent of 'mental perversion' involved in the crime, the court read out the 'entire medical history of the victim—the shattered, perforated intestine caused by the repeated insertion of an iron rod, the tearing of her clothes, looting of her personal belongings and aggravated sexual assault'.

Claps resounded through the courtroom from the visitors' gallery when Justice Misra, along with Justice Ashok Bhushan, sent the twenty-three-year-old paramedic's attackers to the gallows. Justice R. Banumathi, who wrote a separate but concurring judgment, observed that if these convicts did not deserve the death penalty, no others do.

Writing about the incident in the judgment, justices Misra and Bhushan said, 'It sounds like a story from a different world where humanity has been treated with irreverence. The appetite for sex, the hunger for violence, the position of the empowered and the attitude of perversity, to say the least, are bound to shock the collective conscience which knows not what to do.'

Justice Banumathi used equally unforgiving language. 'The present case clearly comes within the category of "rarest of rare case" where the question of any other punishment is unquestionably foreclosed,' the only woman Supreme Court judge wrote. She further elaborated that mitigating considerations like young age and poor background, often cited by the convicts seeking leniency from courts, could not be applied in this case. She said that post-crime remorse and good conduct of the accused, and the absence of criminal antecedents, could not be cited as attenuating considerations to take the case out of the category of the 'rarest of rare cases', adding that in the gang-rape case, 'human lust was allowed to take . . . a demonic form'.

'Where the victims are helpless women, children or

old persons and the accused displayed depraved mentality, committing crime in a diabolic manner, the accused should be shown no remorse and death penalty should be awarded,' Justice Banumathi observed, highlighting that our justice administration system is primarily 'victim-centric'.

The verdict mirrored the revulsion set off by the crime. The judgment was the culmination of the marathon hearings the court held for over a year, as the convicts had appealed against the death penalty awarded to them by the Delhi High Court.

After citing many arguments in the convicts' favour, their lawyers finally attempted to tap the court's mercy by listing out mitigating factors like how they were first-time offenders, were young of age, had young children and aged parents whose lives would become 'calamitous' if they were put to death. The convicts claimed to have reformed, repented and never misbehaved in jail.

The judgment laid primary emphasis on the victim's dying declaration, which was made in gestures, and held that it proved beyond doubt the guilt of the convicts and nailed the case for the police.

The Supreme Court agreed with Delhi Police counsel and senior advocate Siddharth Luthra that anything short of the death penalty would be a 'devastation of social trust'. Luthra had argued that the depravity of the crime invited the 'indignation of society and created a fear psychosis. This case was indeed rarest of rare, considering the brutal and diabolic nature of the crime.'

Despite the protests by the two lawyers who had represented the convicts in the lower court and high court, two senior advocates, Raju Ramachandaran and Sanjay Hegde, were appointed as amicus curiae to defend the convicts. This was to ensure that all the convicts got a proper hearing as there were 'inadequacies' in their arguments.

Collective Conscience

After the Supreme Court's order, several people, including politicians, took to social media to express their support for the judgment.

Speaking on the verdict, Congress president Sonia Gandhi said, 'Four years after the heartbreaking Nirbhaya case that agonised the soul of India, justice has been delivered. I feel deeply for the courageous family of this brave daughter of India who rose to become a symbol of every woman's fight against sexual violence.'

'I am happy that the verdict has been upheld though I wish it had come sooner,' said the Union minister for women and child development Maneka Gandhi.

Congress spokesperson Randeep Surjewala said that 'Nirbhaya's case would remain an example, a deterrent, to all the sexual predators that law and justice for the victims of sexual exploitation and rape will always be delivered, come what may. It is also a reminder to the society and lawmakers to work towards building a safe environment for our women.'

Quoting figures from the National Crime Records Bureau (NCRB), Surjewala said that six women still undergo the trauma of rape in the national capital of Delhi every day and there is a 22 per cent spurt in rapes against women. 'All these are worrisome data and hopefully the government of the day takes note and . . . decisive action,' he said.[2]

'In principle I am against death penalty, but this was such a heinous crime that strictest punishment was needed,' said Brinda Karat of the CPI(M).

BJP's Rajya Sabha MP Subramanian Swamy said, 'It was [a] very tragic incident, which has blotted the civilisation of India. In my opinion there is no doubt whatsoever that all of them were guilty and I think nothing other than capital punishment should be given by the SC.'

A BBC documentary film, *India's Daughter*, written, directed and produced by Leslee Udwin, was released in March 2015. The documentary contained disturbing footage of an interview with one of the rapists, and this prompted the government to block its broadcast. A statement from the home minister's office cited, among other reasons, that clips from the film 'appear to encourage and incite violence against women'.

The film showed an interview in Tihar Jail, Delhi, with one of the accused, Mukesh Singh. His comments regarding the case and the act of rape itself explicitly reflect the traditional misogynistic views inherent in Indian society. 'You can't clap with one hand—it takes two hands. A decent girl won't roam around at night. A girl is more responsible for rape than a boy . . . about 20 per cent of girls are good,' he had said in the interview. 'She should just be silent and allow the rape. Then they would have dropped her off after doing it and only hit the boy.'

The government directed YouTube to block the film in India, and since then BBC has completely taken the video off the site. However, the film has found circulation through various social media outlets and its message continues to be debated by activists, politicians and sexual-abuse survivors around the world.

The collective conscience was hurt, as is evident from the mass protests pan-India and in several other countries. Members of Parliament demanded severe punishment for the perpetrators.

'As a father of three daughters I feel as strongly about the incident as each one of you,' was the sentiment expressed by Manmohan Singh, the then prime minister of India.

Congress president Sonia Gandhi, BJP leader and external affairs minister Sushma Swaraj, former Delhi chief minister Sheila Dixit and former Uttar Pradesh chief minister Mayawati were all unanimous in expressing their anguish. 'Action should be so strict that no one should dare to act in such a manner again,' Mayawati said.[3]

'A new law should be brought in and must get passed to ensure the safety of women,' said Meira Kumar, the then speaker of the Lok Sabha.

The former UN secretary general Ban Ki-moon said that 'violence against women must never be accepted, never excused, never tolerated. Every girl and woman has the right to be respected, valued and protected'.

Author and activist Eve Ensler, the force behind One Billion Rising, a global campaign to end violence against women and girls, said that the incident was a turning point in India and around the world. Ensler, who had travelled to India at the time, said:

Having worked every day of my life for the last 15 years on sexual violence, I have never seen anything like that, where sexual violence broke through the consciousness and was on the front page, nine articles in every paper every day, in the centre of every discourse, in the centre of the college students' discussions, in the centre of any restaurant you went in. [4]

Nirbhaya Act

The barbaric crime led to the enactment of the Criminal Law (Amendment) Bill, 2013, or the Anti-Rape Bill, which was later called the Nirbhaya Act. The new law mandated the death penalty under Section 376(A) of the Indian Penal Code. Under Section 376(A), whoever commits a rape which leads to the death of the victim or causes her to be in a 'persistent vegetative state' shall be punished with rigorous imprisonment for a minimum term of twenty years, which may extend to life imprisonment or even death.

On 22 December 2012, a judicial committee headed by J.S. Verma, a former chief justice of India, was appointed by the Central government to submit a report within thirty days to suggest amendments to criminal law to sternly deal with sexual assault cases.

The late justice Leila Seth (former chief justice of Himachal Pradesh) and Gopal Subramaniam (former solicitor general of India) also presided on the committee. The 631-page report included recommendations on laws related to rape, sexual harassment, trafficking, child sexual abuse, medical examination of victims, and police, electoral and educational reforms.

The committee urged the public in general and particularly eminent jurists, legal professionals, NGOs, women's groups and civil society to share 'their views, knowledge and experience suggesting possible amendments in the criminal and other relevant laws to provide for quicker investigation, prosecution and trial, and also enhanced punishment for criminals accused of committing sexual assault of an extreme nature against women'.

On 26 December 2012, a Commission of Inquiry headed by former Delhi High Court judge Usha Mehra was set up to identify lapses, determine responsibility in relation to the incident, and suggest measures to make Delhi safer for women.

On 3 February 2013, the Criminal Law (Amendment) Ordinance, 2013, was promulgated by the then president Pranab Mukherjee. It provides for the amendment of the Indian Penal Code, Indian Evidence Act and Code of Criminal Procedure, 1973, on laws related to sexual offences. While the amended rape law redefines rape to cover instances of non-penetrative sexual intercourse and increased the age of consent, it is also susceptible to misuse. It also covers instances of consensual sex where girls are below the age of eighteen years, as well as marital rape. In all, the case led to the enactment of much broader rape laws and harsher punishment for the perpetrators of the crime.

The Nirbhaya Trust was established to assist women who have experienced violence to find shelter and legal assistance. 'So many people supported us, so ... we want [to] help those girls who have no one,' said Nirbhaya's father. Nirbhaya Fund is administered by the Department of Economic Affairs,

Ministry of Finance.

Nirbhaya Bhavan, the headquarters of the National Commission for Women, was set up in Jasola, New Delhi. On the foundation-laying ceremony the then president Pranab Mukherjee said: 'Greater sensitization of society is needed to accord due respect to women and we have to work towards ensuring that adequate social awareness is created on women's right and against the evil of barbaric acts of violence and atrocities against women.'

Nirbhaya or Jyoti Singh

In compliance with Indian law, the real name of the victim was initially not released to the media, so pseudonyms were used for her by various media houses instead, including Jagruti (awareness), Jyoti (flame), Amanat (treasure), Nirbhaya (fearless), Damini (lightning) and Delhi's braveheart.

During a protest against the juvenile convict's release on 16 December 2015, the victim's mother said that the victim's name was Jyoti Singh and that she was not ashamed of disclosing it. [5]

Jyoti Singh was born and raised in Delhi while her parents hail from the Ballia district of Uttar Pradesh. Her father had sold his ancestral land to educate her, and worked double shifts to pay for her schooling.

The issues of violence against women and rape have become more salient since the Nirbhaya case. A heightened awareness has led victims to report the crime; police records show that during the final nine months of 2013 almost twice as many rape victims filed a police report and four times as many allegations of molestation were made.

The taboo on discussing rape and sexual violence has been broken. The protests brought debates and discussions on rape to the forefront. There were posters and placards that carried the slogans 'Don't teach us how to dress, teach men not to rape', 'My voice is higher than my skirt', 'Your gaze is the problem so why should I cover myself up?' and 'Don't tell your daughter not to go out, tell your son to behave properly'. All these assertions reflected the changing thinking that violence against women is as much of a men's issue as it is women's.

The media has now started covering sexual violence cases and the police is a little more receptive. Safety and security measures like emergency buttons, GPS technology and CCTVs have been deployed in major cities across the country. The Delhi Transport Corporation (DTC) night-service system increased its capacity from forty-two to eighty-five buses.

However, crimes against women continue to rise. The number of rapes reported by the NCRB in India increased from 24,923 in 2012 to 33,707 in 2013. Compared to other serious crimes like robbery, murder and kidnapping, the rise in the number of rape cases is more dramatic and concerning.

The situation in Delhi, where the Nirbhaya tragedy occurred, has not improved despite the legal reforms. According to 2012 statistics, New Delhi has the highest number of rape reports among all Indian cities.

Rape and the issue of violence against women in general have been endemic to Indian society. The actual number of rapes is far from being recorded, since the unreported figure is extremely high.

There is an enemy in the mind, in our personality, that impedes social change. Social change requires a collective attitudinal change and the replacement of norms. Shared normative beliefs and collective efforts are required to address the issue. Structural, societal and educational reforms are likely to usher in more positive norms.

The Supreme Court's lone woman judge, R. Banumathi, has said the following:

> Stringent legislation and punishment alone may not be sufficient for fighting increasing crime against women. In our tradition-bound society, certain attitudinal change and change in the mindset is needed to respect women and to ensure gender justice. Right from childhood years, children ought to be sensitised to respect women. A child should be taught to respect women in the society in the same way as he is taught to respect men. Gender equality should be made a part of the school curriculum.

Justice Banumathi added that schoolteachers and parents should be trained not only to conduct regular personality-building and skill-enhancing exercises but also to keep a watch on the actual behavioural pattern of children so as to make them gender-sensitized. 'On the practical side, few suggestions are worthwhile to be considered. Use of street lights, illuminated bus stops and extra police patrol during odd hours must be ensured. Police/security guards must be posted at dark and lonely places like parks, streets, etc. Mobile apps for immediate assistance of women should be introduced and effectively maintained,' the judge said, in addition to suggesting that banners and placards be put up inside public transport vehicles. She added that apart from the effective implementation of various legislations protecting women, creating awareness in public on gender justice would go a long way to combat violence against women.

'There are a number of legislations and numerous penal provisions to punish the offenders of violence against women. However, it becomes important to ensure that gender justice does not remain only on paper,' the judge said.

Crimes against women continue to increase despite numerous laws to protect women. Justice Banumathi's judgment asked if laws punishing crimes against women are paper tigers, unable to serve their purpose. 'Offences against women are not women's issue alone but a human rights issue.' She explained that such a brutal incident triggers a sense of dread in society. 'Whenever such grave violations of human dignity come to [the] fore, an unknown sense of insecurity and helplessness grabs the entire society, women in particular, and the only succour people look for, is the State to take command of the situation and remedy it effectively,' she wrote.

While on 5 May the packed courtroom no. 2 of the Supreme Court was resounding with cheer and applause, the next day the Bombay High Court awarded the milder punishment of life imprisonment to the convicts in the similarly horrific gang rape of Bilkis Bano. The Bilkis Bano gang rape occurred after the Godhra riots of 2002. Along with her family, nineteen-year-old Bilkis Bano was escaping a mob in a truck. Bilkis was five months pregnant and accompanying her were seventeen other people in the truck, including her two-year-old daughter. The truck was attacked by an armed mob, who gang-raped her and killed fourteen members of her family, including her daughter and her mother.

The Bano judgment has once again opened the debate on what constitutes the 'rarest of rare case', with many people demanding the grant of the death penalty to those who committed barbaric violence against Bano and murdered her family members.

In 2011, the news of Soumya's rape in Kerala sent shock waves through the country. Soumya was travelling in a train when she was attacked. Her head was smashed and she was thrown out of the train. She was later dragged to the woods and brutally raped by the same man. Soumya eventually succumbed to her injuries.

In 2009, two sisters-in-law went missing from their house in the Shopian district of Jammu and Kashmir. They were raped and murdered and their bodies were recovered barely a kilometre from their home the next day.

Another rape victim, Aruna Shanbaug, died in May 2015 after being in a vegetative state for more than forty years. A nurse by profession, she was raped by a contracted sweeper in 1973. A euthanasia plea, made on her behalf, was rejected by the Supreme Court in 2011 but a landmark judgment, which allowed passive euthanasia in India, was delivered.

'I want no other woman in this city and country to go through such a brutal physical humiliation . . . Perpetrators should be punished . . . they have ruined my life. No punishment short of a life term will take away my pain, humiliation and physical abuse,' commented the twenty-two-year-old photojournalist who was gang-raped by five men in the Shakti Mills Compound, Mahalaxmi, Mumbai, when she was on an assignment.

The NCBR continues to tabulate the rising data. The law has become more stringent. There are a great deal of accountability and safety measures in place. A high degree of sense and sensitivity prevails today. All measures that one expects in a civilized world to create awareness and to curb this menace have been put into force ... however, the abuse still continues.

The abuse still continues ...

3

The 26/11 Mumbai Attacks

Sixty Hours of Terror

'The totality of beliefs and sentiments common to the average members of a society forms a determinate system with a life of its own. It can be termed the collective or creative consciousness.'

—David Émile Durkheim

'Storm the Building'

The Taj Mahal Palace Hotel, a symbol of opulence in Mumbai, lay at the mercy of four heavily armed terrorists. With close to no other options, the government gave orders to storm the building. This started a gun battle which continued for around sixty hours, starting at 9.38 p.m. on 26 November and terminating at 8 a.m. on 29 November.

The carnage ended after the last of nine Pakistani terrorists was killed by the security forces on 29 November 2008. By then a large part of the hotel was in ashes.

The smoke billowing from the front dome of the majestic hotel is etched in the memory of the country. For any serious businessman, foreign investor or wealthy tourist visiting India's commercial capital, the Taj has always been the first choice to stay. The attack on the Taj shook travellers around the world who would have stayed, or were planning to stay, at the iconic property. Moreover, it left a scar on the collective conscience of the entire nation.

The attack did grievous harm to life and property. The Mumbai terror attack claimed 166 lives and injured 238 people. These included policemen, security personnel and foreign nationals. The nation lost thirteen policemen, among whom were two senior Indian Police Service (IPS) officers—Hemant Kamlakar Karkare and Ashok Marutrao Kamte. Property worth Rs 155.57 crore was lost.

The 26/11 Mumbai Terror Attack Case

The case which came to the Court of Sessions for Greater Mumbai dealt with the capture, conviction and hanging of one accused Mohammed Ajmal Amir Kasab.

The Taj Mahal Palace Hotel attack was part of a larger attack on the city. Spread over four days, separate attacks by five pairs of heavily armed terrorists were carried out at various high-profile locations—the Taj, the Oberoi Trident, the Chhatrapati Shivaji Terminus (CST) Railway Station, the Jewish prayer centre at Nariman House, the Metro Cinema and Cama Hospital—as though to wage a war against India. Though the ten terrorists had come together to Mumbai, they carried out attacks in pairs at different locations simultaneously. The two accused who had fired indiscriminately at the Leopold Cafe and Bar at Colaba later joined their two associates, including Kasab, at the Taj.

At 9.38 p.m., a crude RDX bomb was planted in front of the police post near the hotel. Abdul Rehman Bada and Abu Ali, two terrorists armed with AK-47s, ammunition and grenades, made their way to the lobby area of the hotel, firing at anyone and everyone who caught their eye. Next, Abu Shoaib and Abu Umer entered through another door and started shooting down guests in the poolside area.

By midnight, the Mumbai Police had surrounded the Taj. Many of the guests inside the hotel had been huddled up by the staff into small rooms by then. The central dome of the hotel had been bombed and there was a massive fire in the building. The army and firemen arrived at the location.[1]

At the CST the scene was no different. A terrifying bloodbath had ensued, and all that remained were the dead bodies of people who had been unlucky enough to find themselves in the path of the terrorists.

'There is a terrorist attack, *peeche se niklo* [leave through the rear]. *Main hall ke taraf mat jao* [Do not go through the main hall].' Vishnu Dattaram Zende, a prime witness of that fateful evening, made several such announcements and saved a number of lives.

Zende's cabin on the mezzanine floor of the CST was the place from which train announcements were made. He had a completely unobstructed view as he saw two men indiscriminately firing inside the terminus. Kasab and his associate Abu Ismail unleashed this terror on one of the world's busiest railway stations. They went on a killing spree

. . . and there was more to follow.

It was 9.15 p.m. on 26 November 2008. Several people who were on their way home that evening failed to return to their loved ones. The attack lasted for more than twenty-four hours and left fifty-two dead and 109 injured. The firing ended at 10.45 p.m. the next day.

Within an hour of the attack at the CST, two other locations were also attacked—the Leopold Cafe and Bar and the Oberoi Trident Hotel. The Mumbai attack was a war of a unique nature. It was well planned and targeted territories to unleash terror and cause maximum damage. On top of it, it was being orchestrated in real time by conspirators sitting abroad. Hafiz Saeed, the leader of Pakistan's Jama'at-ul-Da'wah, a banned terrorist organization, was accused of being the mastermind behind the attacks. He was giving orders from a location outside India. He also shared tactical advice and guidance through mobile phones as the terrorists carried out the attacks on the city.

The entire country sat shocked in front of their television sets as the attacks unfolded. The government and security forces reacted as quickly as they could. However, they were able to capture only one terrorist alive—Kasab.

There was enough evidence to indict the conspirators in the mass killing of Indians and foreign nationals. They were also accused of destroying property, attempting to instigate communal riots, attempting to falsely portray that the attack was staged by Indian Muslims, and taking foreign nationals and Indians hostage.

Kasab was tried, found guilty and hanged. His trial sparked a long-drawn-out debate over capital punishment. A section of society opposed his hanging, saying that the national conscience could not be satisfied by executing him and that his execution would instead lead to more violence. However, the majority held the view that the crime, given its magnitude, warranted the death penalty.

Kasab's Confession

Kasab's confession was recorded by Sawant Wagule, additional chief metropolitan magistrate, Mumbai. 'Were you ill-treated or abused by the police? Why do you want to make this confessional statement?'—these were some of the questions she put to Kasab as she carried out the proceedings.

Wagule ensured that Kasab was making the confessional statement voluntarily and not under pressure, coercion or allurement by the police. He was remanded to judicial custody to reflect on this for a day, during which he was not accessible to the police or any other agency. According to the norms, the next day, the magistrate again confirmed that Kasab wanted to make the confessional statement of his own volition and not under anyone's influence.

While confessing, he did not show any feelings of guilt or remorse. 'I have absolutely no regrets about carrying out this attack and I am making this confession to set an example for others to become like me and follow my actions . . .' There was clarity in what Kasab uttered. Wagule listened patiently to what he had to say while cautioning him that any confessional statement made by him would be used as evidence that might lead to his conviction. Two days later, the judge repeated the entire gamut of cautions before proceeding to record Kasab's statement under Section 164 of the Code of Criminal Procedure (CrPC). Under the provision, a confession or statement given voluntarily by an accused or any other person is recorded by a metropolitan or judicial magistrate. The judicial officer explains to the person making it that the confessional statement may be used against him or her. This helps to strengthen the case of the prosecution, reduces the chances of witnesses turning hostile and serves as a check against any tampering of evidence.

Once all procedures had been adhered to, Kasab began his confession: 'On 26 November 2008, we [my accomplice and I] made a fidayeen attack [suicide attack] on Mumbai city,' he said. 'This confession is about the attack and the conspiracy behind it.'

Journey to Mumbai

At noon on 23 November, Kasab and his nine Pakistani associates, with an intention to undertake a fidayeen attack in India, had started from Karachi Creek in a small boat named *Al-Hussaini*, which they abandoned near Porbandar. The next day, in the afternoon, they captured an Indian fishing trawler named *Kuber* on the pretext of seeking help. The ten fidayeen boarded the *Kuber* and forced its navigator Amarchand Solanki to head for Mumbai. As per Kasab's confession:

I took the *nakhva* [navigator] to the engine room and tied his hands and legs and covered his eyes with a black strip. I slit the neck of the nakhva with a knife and killed him on arrival. I have hidden the nakhva's dead body in the boat.

We have kept our satellite phone, GPS and notebook in the boat and have left the boat in the sea.

Equipped with arms and ammunitions, bombs and grenades, the terrorists then left the *Kuber* at a distance of four nautical miles from Mumbai and set off for the shore in a dinghy (rubber boat) which they carried from Pakistan. They were even carrying dry fruit for nourishment during the attacks. After sailing for nearly two hours, they reached Badhwar Park around 9 p.m.

The Attack on the CST and Kasab's Capture

Kasab and Ismail were running ninety minutes behind schedule. They took a taxi and reached the CST in twenty minutes. Once inside the terminus, they placed a bomb among the passengers' luggage, took out AK-47s from their bags and started firing indiscriminately.

The duo emerged from the railway station shooting at whoever crossed their path. Their killing spree at the CST had left sixty people dead. They then tried to flag a taxi on Badruddin Tayabji Marg. By now, heavy police firing had started and they took shelter on the terrace of the Cama & Albless Hospital, to which they had climbed.

Before entering the hospital, the terrorist duo did something chilling. Ismail saw one Thakur Waghela having dinner with his four-year-old son outside his shanty in a lane outside the hospital. He and Kasab approached the unsuspecting Waghela for a glass of water, and were quickly obliged. After Kasab finished drinking the water, he shot a bullet through Waghela's chest. His four-year-old son Niraj saw his father being killed through the opening of the bathroom door.[2] Waghela's mother, Jamuna, who escaped death by a whisker on that fateful night, had warned her son not to have his dinner outside the shanty.[3] The terrorists also fired at another person before jumping over a closed entrance into the hospital.

It was later, outside the hospital, that Kasab opened fire on some of the country's most decorated brave hearts—the then chief of Mumbai's Anti-terrorism Squad (ATS) Hemant Karkare, Additional Commissioner of Police (ACP) Ashok Kamte and Anti-extortion Cell Chief and encounter specialist Vijay Salaskar. They died in the ensuing gun battle before the two fidayeen fled in the snatched Toyota Qualis of the slain police officers.

The terrorist duo then drove to the Metro Cinema junction. Here, they started firing at a parked police vehicle, killing Arun Raghunath Chitte, Salaskar's driver. Though Chitte was not with his boss that night, both him and Salaskar were killed by the same terrorists within minutes of each other. Chitte had joined the Mumbai Police in 1995 as a driver and had spent ten years in service as Salaskar's driver.[4]

Kasab and his accomplice were finally intercepted when they approached Inspector Sanjay Govilkar and Assistant Sub-inspector Tukaram Gopal Omble at Vinoli Chowpatty in their stolen car on 26 November 2008. In the gunfight that followed, Govilkar shot Ismail Khan fatally and injured Kasab. Kasab had managed to fire bullets into Assistant Sub-inspector Omble's chest. Badly shot and totally unarmed, Omble grappled with Kasab and didn't let go, before other members of the force finally overpowered the terrorist.[5] Unfortunately, the bullet wounds proved fatal, and Omble lost his life. He was awarded the Ashoka Chakra posthumously for his valour.

The moment they captured Kasab, Govilkar and his colleagues started beating him up with their lathis. However, Govilkar immediately saw that Kasab would be more valuable alive and asked his colleagues to stop. It was this timely wisdom and presence of mind that would earn him the applause of his seniors and prove crucial in uncovering the machinations of the terrorists. 'I am proud that I was part of the team that caught him alive . . . I always wanted to be a policeman and that day I was wearing my uniform, it gave me a unique courage,' he later told the media. In his daredevil fight to capture the terrorist, the young inspector hadn't even realized that he had been shot.

The fidayeen duo was brought to Nair Hospital in an ambulance. In hospital, Kasab learnt that Ismail had succumbed to his injuries. Kasab gave his and Ismail's names to the police and confirmed that they were Pakistanis. His statement led to the recovery of the Indian boat *Kuber*, the body of its navigator, Solanki, the satellite phone and the GPS.

Operation Black Tornado

Back at the Taj Mahal Palace Hotel, the National Security Guard (NSG) had launched Operation Black Tornado. Commando Major Sandeep Unnikrishnan was the first NSG officer to die in combat. On 28 November at 1 a.m., thirty-one-year-old Unnikrishnan led his team up the grand staircase to the sixth floor of the Taj. The courageous officer was able to rescue fourteen hostages from the clutches of the terrorists, before he succumbed to the bullets injuries he received while fighting the terrorists. His last message to the men carrying out the operation under him has now become a hallmark of his bravery: 'Do not come up, I will handle them.'

NSG commando Havildar Gajender Singh died a hero's death while leading his team to flush the other two terrorists—Imran Babar and Nasir alias Abu Umer—out of Nariman House, the orthodox Jewish centre in Mumbai. The officer, who also took part in the Kargil War, had always wanted to die in a battle defending his country.[6] Based in Delhi, he was on deputation from the Indian Army's Special Forces Parachute Regiment to the NSG's 51 Special Action Group and was sent to Mumbai on the night of the attacks.

The six bravehearts who died fighting terrorists were all conferred with the Ashoka Chakra, the country's highest peacetime gallantry medal, by President Pratibha Patil. These heroes included Maharashtra ATS chief Hemant Karkare, ACP Ashok Kamte, Inspector Vijay Salaskar, Assistant Sub-inspector Tukaram Omble, and NSG commandos Major Sandeep Unnikrishnan and Havildar Gajender Singh.

The Making of a Terrorist

The court case mentions the details of Kasab's early days. They give us a hint as to why he chose to become a terrorist and unleashed such a brutal terror attack on an entire city.

Kasab had studied up to the fourth standard in an

Urdu-medium school in Faridkot village in Pakistan's Punjab province. After dropping out of school in 2000, he worked as a labourer in Lahore and later with a tent service.

In November 2007, both Kasab and one Muzaffar Lal Khan had left for Rawalpindi in search of better employment. As per Kasab:

> One day we saw members of the Lashkar-e-Taiba going from door to door under the name of Jama'at-ul-Da'wah, collecting the hides of goats sacrificed on Eid-ul-Zoha. They were asking people to donate the hides to help achieve independence for Kashmir. The whole idea appealed to me. I became interested in fighting for the liberation of Kashmir. I was inspired and wanted to be a part of it.

Soon he attended three training camps where he received lessons in jihad and arms and ammunitions. Before he left for Mumbai, the terrorist had become well versed in dismantling and assembling AK-47 rifles and pistols, operating rocket launchers and using hand grenades. 'I also received training in the use of satellite phones and GPS systems . . . Marine training made me adept at reading and using maps, fathoming the depths of the sea, using GPS for marine ways, casting fishing nets and sailing.'

The Trial and the Verdict

Kasab's disclosure statement led to the search for the *Kuber* and the dead body of the Indian navigator Solanki. Kasab also helped retrieve a satellite phone, a GPS and a notebook that were concealed under a wooden plank in the engine room. The forensic team carried out DNA tests to ascertain the identities of the dead terrorists from the clothes found in the boat.

Everything indicated that they were from Pakistan—the routes taken by the *Kuber* and the rubber dinghy itself, and the devices recovered from the terrorists. The routes showed that the terrorists had made their way to India by sea from Pakistan via Gujarat near Porbandar (where the *Kuber* had been hijacked) and then to south Mumbai. The Yamaha outboard motor of the rubber dinghy was established to have been dispatched to a vendor in Karachi, Pakistan, from Japan.

The telephone intercepts of conversations between the terrorists and their collaborators in Pakistan were proof enough that the other side of the border had played a role in the attack. Various deceptive and masking devices had been used to try and show that the terrorists' interlocutors had Indian names and were located in the United States.

Some of the major charges against Kasab were conspiracy to wage war; commission of terrorist acts; committing murder of a number of persons; and causing explosions punishable under the Explosive Substance Act, 1908.

Two other accused, Fahim Ansari and Sabauddin Ahmed, both Indian nationals, were arraigned before the trial court and indicted on the same charges as the Pakistani terrorist.

This is the first case in Indian history where the court allowed the accused, who was not an Indian citizen, to be represented by a lawyer. Going by the Constitution of India, the Mumbai court also gave Kasab a lawyer. Initially, Abbas Kazmi, a criminal lawyer, was appointed by the trial judge on 16 April 2009 to represent Kasab, but he left the trial midway. Later, Kasab was represented by two other lawyers, Anjali Waghmare and K.P. Pawar.

At the end of the trial, Kasab was found guilty on all counts and was awarded the death sentence on five counts, life sentence on five other counts and a number of relatively lighter sentences of imprisonment for the other offences. He was convicted and sentenced to death by Special Judge M.L. Tahaliyani on 6 May 2010. The other two accused were acquitted of all charges as the trial judge gave them the benefit of the doubt and also held that the prosecution completely failed to establish conspiracy and other charges against them.

The judgment by the trial court led to a reference to the Bombay High Court under Section 366 of the CrPC. Two cross-appeals (when both the parties to the case challenge the judgment) came to the high court (HC), one by Kasab against his conviction and sentences, and the other by the State of Maharashtra against the acquittal of the other two accused. The HC bench comprising justices Ranjana Desai and R.V. More confirmed the death sentences awarded to Kasab on 21 February 2011, but did not interfere with the acquittal of the other two accused. Kasab, through his counsel Amin Solkar, had conveyed to the HC that he wanted to remain present in the court during the hearing, but considering the threat perception expressed by the Maharashtra Police his request was turned down on 20 September 2010. The HC, however, directed the state to make arrangements for videoconferencing so that Kasab could see the court proceedings and hear the arguments.

The Supreme Court Verdict

Two appeals were filed in the Supreme Court (SC): a jail appeal by Kasab and the other by the State of Maharashtra. Kasab was unrepresented in the appeal written by him from jail. He was allowed every avenue provided by the law to defend himself. Here, the apex court named senior advocate Raju Ramachandran amicus curiae and appointed him to represent Kasab.

After a marathon hearing, spanning over two and a half months, on 29 August 2012, the Supreme Court upheld the death penalty awarded to Kasab for waging war against India. It also upheld the acquittal of two alleged Indian co-conspirators.

'In the rarest of rare cases', when the collective conscience is so shocked, it is expected that the judges will award or retain the death penalty irrespective of their personal opinions, the apex court said. A bench comprising justices Aftab Alam and C.K. Prasad ruled that the case had the element of conspiracy as no other case and the Pakistani terrorist was part of a conspiracy hatched on the other side of the border to wage war against the Government of India.

In the written judgment, Justice Alam said:

The conspiracy was to launch a murderous attack on Mumbai, regarding it as the financial centre of the country . . . It has a magnitude of unprecedented enormity on all scales. The conspiracy . . . was deep and large as it was vicious. In terms of loss of life and property, and more importantly in its traumatizing effect, this case stands alone, or it is at least the very rarest of rare to come before this court since the birth of the Republic. Therefore, it should also attract the rarest of rare punishments.

Ramachandran's basic premise after going through Kasab's case was as follows: 'Kasab's culpability should be judged, and commensurate punishment for him should be determined only on the basis of the offences directly attributable to him.' He wanted to confine the case only to acts committed by Kasab and his dead accomplice Ismail from the time the two arrived at Badhwar Park until they were caught at Vinoli Chowpatty.

Senior counsel and former solicitor general Gopal Subramanium, appearing for the State of Maharashtra, had expressed his shock at Ramachandran's contention to treat the case in isolation. 'Kasab was a member of a close knit team of ten terrorists who arrived together in Mumbai and attacked their various targets in furtherance of a common conspiracy,' he lamented, adding that a much larger and ominous conspiracy was hatched with the aim to destabilize the country. He held that the attacks at all locations were integrally connected with each other and that Kasab and Ismail were as much a part of the offences committed at the other places as they were responsible for the offences committed by them directly. Sensing that the first argument could not be effected, Ramachandran challenged Subramanium's acumen by citing procedural lapses, an equally important feature that according to him was not given due consideration.

The amicus curiae contended that the right to a fair trial was an integral part of the right to life and personal liberty guaranteed by Article 21 of the Constitution. Ramachandran argued that in Kasab's case the guarantee remained unsatisfied because two constitutional rights had been denied to him: the right to counsel at the earliest;[7] and the right to protection against self-incrimination.[8]

Ramachandran argued that Kasab was not made aware of his right to counsel at the time of his arrest and when he was produced before the judicial magistrate during the remand proceedings. He stressed upon the fact that a mere offer of legal aid was not the same as being made aware that an accused had the constitutional right to consult and be defended by a legal practitioner.

There was a slight murmur in the courtroom and before any tacit approval was made, Ramachandran went on, 'Until Kasab was produced before the additional chief metropolitan magistrate for recording his confession, he was not informed of such a right . . . The magistrate did not tell Kasab that he had the fundamental right to consult and be represented by a lawyer, but simply asked him whether he wanted one.'

Kasab had written two letters in which he sought the help of the Pakistani High Commission to provide him with a Pakistani lawyer. Ramachandran submitted that Kasab wanted a Pakistani lawyer and, therefore, it was the duty of the court either to make arrangements for him to be represented by a Pakistani lawyer or to tell him clearly that his request could not be acceded to and that if he wished he could be provided with adequate legal representation. Ramachandran argued that apart from the constitutional and legal principles, the rules of natural justice demanded that the accused be so informed.

The senior counsel further raised the issue that Kasab's confessional statement was not voluntary but tutored to suit the prosecution's case. He said that the statement was too long and had too many unnecessary details. 'A person making a confession with regard to the attack would normally not go into all the unnecessary particulars on his own unless prompted by some external agency,' he pointed out.

Ramachandran finally added due process had been compromised during Kasab's trial and, therefore, he should not be given the death sentence. His strongest argument for not awarding the death penalty to Kasab was his age, besides poverty and his educational background, which had driven him to this bloodshed. He was lured by a group of fanatic murderers seemingly engaged in social work, Ramachandran said, adding that Kasab had actually wanted to contribute towards helping the Kashmiris, whom he was led to believe were oppressed by the Indian government.

'It would appear wholly unjust to give the death penalty to Kasab. The death penalty should be kept reserved for his handlers, who, unfortunately, are not before a court till now.'

However, his attempts were rendered futile. A calm and composed Subramanium stood up and, with a fleeting smile, he tore into Ramachandran's argument. 'All constitutional rights of Kasab, including the right to be defended by a lawyer and protection against self-incrimination, were fully secured and upheld by courts,' he said.

Kasab's refusal to accept the services of an Indian lawyer and his demand for a lawyer from his country was his own independent decision, he said, adding that the demand for a Pakistani lawyer could not have been possible especially when

Pakistan was denying that Kasab was even a Pakistani citizen. Besides, argued Subramanium, Kasab certainly did not need any advice from an Indian court or authority as he was acting quite independently and was, in his mind, a 'patriotic' Pakistani at war with this country. The senior lawyer added, while apprising the judges, that Kasab was immediately provided with a set of two lawyers after he was convinced that no help was pouring in from Pakistan or anywhere else.

Subramanium facilitated a chart showing not only the day-to-day developments in the trial but also giving details of the hours of the court proceedings on each day to assert that Kazmi had been given ample time to prepare his defence against submissions made by Special Public Prosecutor Ujjwal Nikam.

Even Kazmi himself, who raised all kinds of objections and left no opportunity to noisily protest against the procedural decisions of the trial court, never complained about not being given sufficient time for preparation, the former Solicitor General stated, adding that his requests for adjournment were accommodated by the court on most occasions.

Watan Parast

The SC refused to accept that Kasab was a mere tool in the hands of the terrorist organization Lashkar-e-Taiba. It noted that the terrorist joined the organization around December 2007 and continued as its member till the end despite a number of opportunities to leave it.

'This shows his clear and unmistakable intention to be a part of the organization and participate in its designs. Even after his arrest he regarded himself as a "watan parast", a patriotic Pakistani at war with this country,' the judgment stated.

Then the judges went on to say:

> It is true that he is not educated but he is a very good and quick learner, has a tough mind and strong determination. He is also quite clever and shrewd. Unfortunately, he is wholly remorseless and any feeling of pity is unknown to him . . . He kills without the slightest twinge of conscience . . . The saddest and the most disturbing part of the case is that Kasab never showed any remorse for the terrible things he did.

According to Justice Alam, Kasab made the confessional statement not out of any sense of guilt, sorrow or grief but to present himself as a hero. He told the magistrate that he had absolutely no regret for whatever he had done and he wanted to make the confession to set an example for others to become a fidayeen like him and follow him in his deeds, the judge noted, while delving deep into the parameters of 'the rarest of rare cases' to decide upon the harshest punishment.

Noting that he was never repentant and did not show any sign of contrition, the SC felt that he had no potential for reform and rehabilitation, thus concluding that death remained the only punishment that could be given to him.

Other broad guidelines for awarding the death sentence were also taken into consideration. Among these were the brutal and dastardly manner in which the murders were committed, the magnitude of the crime and its antisocial or socially abhorrent nature, and the helpless victims.

The SC complimented all those who showed great presence of mind and professionalism and, caring little for their own safety, saved countless lives or photographed the terrorists on their killing spree, thus providing unimpeachable evidence to the court. In the course of the hearing of the case, which was spread over thirteen weeks, not once were voices raised, not once was the counsel of the other side interrupted and contradicted on a statement of fact and the points of law were debated in a congenial atmosphere.

Ramachandran accepted the SC verdict, saying, 'I bow to the verdict of the court . . . No lawyer should be attached to the result of the case . . . Let us all take pride in our judicial system.' Ramachandran termed the Kasab case to be one of the greatest professional challenges of his career, which he dealt with to the best of his abilities:

> I would definitely call it one of the greatest professional challenges of my career to be able to make plausible arguments in a case which the world has thought to be hopeless. I think the court has given anxious consideration to various submissions made on behalf of the accused and that is a matter of satisfaction . . . [Appointing me amicus] was an honour given to me. I took it as a sacred duty.[9]

Kasab, the only terrorist tried for the massacre of 164 people during the 26/11 Mumbai terror attacks, was hanged to death on 21 November 2012 at Pune's Yerwada prison in a hush-hush operation. His mercy petition was rejected by the President on 5 November 2012. The Indian High Commission in Islamabad had informed the Pakistan government about Kasab's hanging through a letter. But when Pakistan refused to receive the letter, they were communicated through fax.

It was only when he was being taken to the gallows that Kasab lost his composure. Otherwise he sang songs in his cell even after he was told about his execution. He also expressed an unusual desire for tomatoes in the morning and ate one in the morning before his execution. However, his last wish to meet his family could not be fulfilled as the Pakistan government did not respond even after it was informed about the hanging. Kasab was buried in an open space near the *faansi* (gallows) gate. Six pits were kept ready to ensure that the exact burial spot remained a secret.[10]

The defence lawyers—Amin Solkar, Farhana Shah and Abbas Kazmi—who appeared for the Pakistani gunman in the sessions court and Bombay High Court welcomed his execution and hoped that it would bring some closure and peace to the victims of the terror attack. 'It is good that the government expedited this case ... Maybe guarding him for so long was becoming a burden on the exchequer,' Solkar said, while raising questions about the secrecy. He also found support from Shah who defended Kasab in the HC. 'Why was the execution shrouded in such secrecy?'[11]

The Collective Conscience

The Mumbai attacks had the element of conspiracy and the magnitude of unprecedented enormity on all scales—viciousness, ruthlessness and trauma. Unlike any other case, the planning and preparation had been meticulous and detailed, with extensively trained combatants, clear instructions, predetermined targets, and harmless and defenceless victims. The number of policemen and members of security forces killed and injured in the course of their duty would hardly find a match in any other case.

Kasab was part of a conspiracy hatched across the border to launch a murderous attack on Mumbai—to kill as many Indians and foreign nationals as possible, to take them as hostages and use them as bargaining chips to further the terrorists' demands, and to incite communal strife and insurgency. This was done with the intent to weaken the country from within. He and his accomplices killed and injured people simply because they happened to be Indians. The court maintained that this case had shocked the collective conscience of the people of India.

Ten-year-old Devika Rotawan was the youngest witness in the case. She was shot in the leg by Kasab at the CST on the night of 26/11 and had identified him. Rotawan, along with her father and brother, were waiting at the CST to board a train to Pune when she was shot. She wanted him to be hanged along with the masterminds behind the gruesome attack. 'There was chaos as the terrorists fired and like everybody else, we ran to find shelter. There was chaos and before we could realize what was happening, I was shot,' she said. The little girl had to undergo multiple surgeries to be able to walk again. Now the brave teenager is determined to join the Indian Police Service. 'The first time I was the victim, the next time I will be the saviour,' she added.[12]

The public reaction to Kasab's death sentence was not entirely one-sided. A majority of people celebrated the verdict, with the Shiv Sena going to the extent of distributing sweets. 'This is a tribute to the people and police officers who lost their lives during the attack,' said R.R. Patil, Maharashtra's home minister.

People across the country debated profusely on two main questions: Is the verdict going to send a strong message across the world on India's stand on terrorism? Is the verdict going to bring about the desired change?

There was a mixed reaction from the Pakistani media, with a section saying that it should help the victims' families to put a lid on an 'ugly chapter', while another warned that it 'will impact' Indo-Pak ties. 'Like it or not, there are fundamental issues between the two countries that have to be resolved; but by holding everything hostage to the terrorism issue, India may have in fact given the terrorists a perverse incentive to try harder the next time,' the Pakistani publication *Dawn* warned in an editorial.[13]

Kasab was viewed by many as a mere puppet. While India has backed the death penalty at the United Nations along with other countries that still carry out capital punishment, at home there are varying positions on the issue. Death as a penalty has been held to be constitutionally valid, though it is indeed to be awarded in the 'rarest of rare cases when the alternative option (of life sentence) is unquestionably foreclosed'.

Speaking on the death sentence, Devansh Mohta, one of the lawyers who assisted Subramanium in the case, holds that capital punishment has lost its deterrence value in general. 'Therefore, its retention serves no purpose. However, in a civil society, since there is no higher punishment that the judiciary can provide against terrorism, capital punishment must be retained but only in such cases.' Even human rights groups have renewed calls for India to abolish capital punishment.

For several reasons, the hanging of Kasab was termed an act of vengeance. Some oppose state executions for whatever the crime may be. Eminent social activist Medha Patkar called the concept of death penalty 'unfortunate' as she believes that the 'state does not have the right to take anyone's life, irrespective of the crime committed'.

Others feel that terrorists like Kasab deserve death since they themselves do not believe in human rights and human values. They shouldn't expect nor do they deserve any better. They also say that Kasab was accorded the due process of law and his culpability in the heinous crimes—which certainly fall into the 'rarest of rare' category for which capital punishment can be awarded—has been proved beyond the shadow of a doubt.

An Attack That Shook an Entire Nation

The country has witnessed a number of terrorist attacks since Independence, but the worst among all was the Mumbai terror attacks. A world in shock watched the terrorists systematically kill 166 people, maim and injure another 238, and damage and destroy ten target locations. The attackers killed mostly Indians, in addition to singling out westerners, particularly Americans, the British and Israelis. A total of twenty-six foreign nationals were killed.

Up until the Mumbai carnage, terror was associated with dreadful attacks on the common man. This attack showed that everyone, despite socio-economic standing, is vulnerable to such attacks. This one especially targeted foreign nationals to ensure that the one was felt globally and not just by one nation. This had significant international ramifications for the country.

The Taj Mahal Palace Hotel, the vibrant economic hub, was under siege for more than sixty hours. Constant shootings and bombings led to large plumes of smoke engulfing the front dome of the iconic hotel property. This also created panic and nerve-wracking fear among hundreds of people trapped inside. The 26/11 image of the Taj still lingers on. The attack on the hotel symbolized something way more powerful.[14]

The hotel's interiors were charred, walls were marred by bullet holes and grenade blasts, and its corridors were soaked in blood. It took close to two years before the Taj Mahal Palace reopened in its entirety on 15 August 2010, India's Independence Day. Certain sections of the luxury hotel had opened just twenty-one days after the attack amidst tightened security. Nearly 270 rooms in the tower wing of the Taj Mahal Palace and Tower, nine suites and twenty-six club rooms were made available for guests.

The Oberoi Trident, the other icon of luxury and opulence in Mumbai, also witnessed the gory incidents. By the time the siege ended, 143 hostages were rescued alive and twenty-four bodies were recovered from the hotel.

The largest significance of 26/11 lay in the impact that it had on public emotion. Never before had a terrorist attack given rise to public debate on the role played by every element of society in inhibiting terror.

The spirit of Mumbai still exists, but the old bravado

is gone—replaced by an air of precaution. The people of Maximum City feel more vulnerable to the possibility of such attacks in the future. Kamal Singh, a witness of the attack on Nariman House, said his community was even considering arming themselves because, if an attack happens again, 'we have to learn to face it without the police'.[15]

Sunita Shah, who was at the CST on 26/11, summed up how people have come to terms with the fact that they will never have security: 'Mumbai is attacked so often that one just becomes numb to it. Not much seems to have changed. The people certainly don't feel safer. We are just waiting for the next tragedy.'

4

The Babri Masjid Demolition

The Conflict of Faith

'I heard a thousand blended notes,
While in a grove I sat reclined,
In that sweet mood when pleasant thoughts
Bring sad thoughts to the mind.
To her fair works did Nature link
The human soul that through me ran;
And much it grieved my heart to think
What man has made of man.'

—William Wordsworth

If there is a day that post-Independence India will never forget, it is 6 December 1992. On that day, Hindu *kar sevaks* (activists) stormed Babri Masjid, a sixteenth-century mosque built by the first Mughal emperor Babur's Shia army commander, Mir Baqi. The mob of kar sevaks demolished the constructed portion, the boundary wall, the Ram Chabutra and some other portions in the disputed premises of the Babri Masjid in the city of Ayodhya, Uttar Pradesh.

A makeshift temple was constructed under the central dome and the idol of Ram Lalla (the infant Lord Ram) was placed there. The kar sevaks had achieved their objective, which was to install the Hindu deity back in its place and establish their physical right over the disputed site after four and a half centuries. They claimed that the mosque was built on land considered holy by Hindus, who believed it to be the birthplace of Lord Rama.

Although it has never been proven, the wide consensus—based on evidence stretching across centuries—is that the mosque was built in 1528 on the orders of the Mughal emperor Babur. Hindus believe it was at this place that an ancient temple from Maharaja Vikramaditya's time existed and that Babur's army pulled it down to erect the Babri Masjid. A piece of land measuring 17' x 21' (33.11 square metres) had been the cause of discontentment between the Hindu and Muslim communities.

The demolition, which took place in spite of the Supreme Court's order that no damage should be caused to the disputed structure, triggered massive communal riots across the country and at least 2000 people were killed. A number of senior BJP leaders, including L.K. Advani and Dr Murli Manohar Joshi, were accused of inciting the kar sevaks. The demolition also resulted in the dismissal of the Kalyan Singh–led BJP government in Uttar Pradesh. But nevertheless, the BJP came to power in the late 1990s under Prime Minister Atal Bihari Vajpayee.

Kalyan Singh recently owned full responsibility for the

demolition of the sixteenth-century mosque, saying, 'As the chief minister of UP, I had ordered police not to fire at Ram bhakts who had assembled at Ayodhya in 1992 during the Ram temple movement, which led to demolition of the Babri mosque. I take full responsibility.'[1]

———

The issue of the Babri Masjid goes back to 1885 when both Hindus and Muslims laid claims over a disputed premises constructed before the eighteenth century. The dispute at the time led to communal riots in the district of Faizabad.

The dispute started over a 1250-square-metre premises in the Faizabad district of Ayodhya. The premises consisted of a constructed portion and adjoining land surrounded by a boundary wall, which was undisputedly constructed before the eighteenth century. This area was used for worship in Ayodhya. While Muslims claimed that the entire premises constituted the Babri mosque, they admitted that the outer part of the adjoining land had a *chabutra* or platform (39.6 square yards in size) towards the south-east where Hindus had worshipped since the middle of the nineteenth century. On the other hand, Hindus claimed that they had been worshipping there since time immemorial. These rival claims have been judicially recorded since 1885.

The issue was first triggered when Muslims started asserting their right over a nearby temple, Hanuman Garhi, near the Babri Masjid in 1855. They claimed that it used to be a mosque, a stand rejected by Hindus. This led to riots, with the fight continuing till Hindus retreated from the disputed premises. Hundreds of people were injured and several lost their lives. Those who were killed during the riots were buried around the disputed premises.

Soon after the riots, the adjoining land was divided almost equally into two parts by an 8-feet-high brick-and-iron grill wall. Muslims were supposed to use the inner portion and Hindus the outer portion towards the east. This was done to maintain peace between the two communities. The railing/grill was erected around 1956. Initially there was only one door in the boundary wall towards the east. Later, around 1877, another door was opened towards the north. Hindus were given control and management of the gate by the government authorities, despite severe objections by Muslims.

Since a large number of Hindu devotees would gather to worship at the chabutra twice a year, two doors were allowed to be operated so as to control the crowd—one for entry and the other for exit. Muslims had objected to this too. Ultimately a fragile truce was arrived at and it was agreed that the exact place of worship must be marked by some neutral European officer. This was an attempt to accord sanctity and to curtail the growing discontentment. It was accordingly done.

It was in 1885 that for the first time a suit was filed by plaintiff Mahant Raghubar Dasmahant of the Janmasthan situated in Ayodhya, against the Secretary of State for India in Council; he sought permission to construct a temple over the Ram Chabutra (measuring 17' x 21') as it was the sacred place of Hindus. He also sought to prevent Muslims from interfering in the construction process.

One Mohammad Ashgar had filed an impleadment and opposed the petition. Ashgar in his written statement mentioned that it was Babur who had constructed the mosque and that on the outer door (the eastern one) the word 'Allah' was inscribed; thereafter, the statement held, there was no question of ownership by any other person, hence the mahant was not the owner of the chabutra or the land underneath. Ashgar said there was no document on record to entitle the plaintiff to construct the temple. He further stated that by merely going inside part of the mosque, Hindus could not claim any right as very often non-Muslims visited *imambara*s, mosques and graves for making offerings and Muslims did not prohibit them. Ashgar told the court that the chabutra was constructed in 1857 and Hindus were permitted to visit the chabutra subject to certain conditions, one of which was that no new construction should be made. It was further stated that whenever the plaintiff or some other Hindus had intended to do something new inside the compound of the mosque, the government had stopped them. Even a monk's thatch placed there was removed. However, Muslims did not deny the correctness of the map filed along with the plaint. During the pendency of the matter, another map was prepared, which also substantially tallied with the first one filed by the mahant.

On 24 December 1885, after the perusal of the two maps, the Faizabad sub-judge in his judgment, written in Urdu, held that there was no doubt regarding the possession and ownership of Hindus over the chabutra, which had *charan*s (feet) embossed on it and an idol of Thakurji installed on it. Besides, these articles were being worshipped by Hindus. He further held that the pukka grill wall between the mosque and the chabutra served as a dividing line between the two.

Noting that near the chabutra was the mosque wall and the word 'Allah' was inscribed on it, the trial judge ruled that it would be against public policy to permit the construction of the temple, as the sound of bells and the shankh, common to Hindu rituals, would lead to greater conflict when Muslims passed that way; greater conflict could lead to another riot and the massacre of thousands of people. Ultimately, the judge opined that granting permission to construct the temple would amount to laying down the foundation of a riot between the two communities. Thus, the suit was dismissed.

Later, in March 1886, F.E.A. Chamier, district judge, Faizabad, visited the disputed land and found that the mosque stood on the border of the town of Ayodhya. In his judgment, he observed that 'it is most unfortunate that a masjid should have been built on land especially held sacred by the Hindus, but as that event occurred 356 years ago it is too late now to remedy the grievance. All that can be done is to maintain the parties in status quo.' The district judge struck out the words holding the ownership of Hindus over the chabutra from the previous judgment.

Justice W. Young, judicial commissioner, Oudh, in his judgment also observed that Hindus seem to have got very limited rights of access to certain spots within the precincts adjoining the mosque. For years, Hindus tried persistently to increase their rights and to erect buildings on two spots in the enclosure—Sita Ki Rasoi (Sita's kitchen) and Ram Chandar Ki Janmabhoomi (Lord Rama's birthplace). Justice Young further noted that the executive authorities had repeatedly rejected the construction of these encroachments and had absolutely forbidden any alteration of the status quo. 'I think this is a very wise and proper procedure on their part and I am further of opinion that the Civil Courts have properly dismissed the plaintiff's claim,' he wrote. So the status quo continued till December 1949.

The Incident of 23 December 1949

In the early hours of 23 December 1949, around 4 a.m., two idols, one of Lord Rama and the other of his consort, goddess Sita, appeared inside the mosque—supposedly put there by Hindus. It was alleged that around fifty people broke the locks on the compound of the Babri Masjid, climbed the walls, trespassed into the mosque and placed the idols in the *janmasthan* (place of birth). The Nirmohi Akhara was said to have possessed the temple. Afterwards, a crowd of 5000 people collected and raised religious slogans and performed puja. It led to widespread protests; consequently, the government declared the site disputed and locked the gates on 29 December 1949. The additional city magistrate, Faizabad-cum-Ayodhya, after attaching the disputed site, placed it under the management of Sri Priya Datt Ram, chairman, municipal board. Priya Datt continued to worship the deity of Bhagwan Sri Ram Lala Virajmaan under the central dome. However, from then onwards, Muslims were prohibited from entering the building premises.

In 1950, Mahant Paramhans Ramchandra Das, the chief of the Ram Janmabhoomi Nyas, and Gopal Singh Visharad filed suits in the Faizabad court asking for the right to worship the idols installed at the 'Asthan Janmabhoomi'. Nirmohi Akhara, one of the main parties in the dispute, and others filed a suit in 1959 seeking permission to hold prayer ceremonies again.

Even the Sunni Central Waqf Board led by Hashim Ansari in Uttar Pradesh filed a suit in 1961, staking its claim to the Babri Masjid and adjoining graveyard. While Muslim organizations sought the restoration of the disputed shrine to Muslims, Hindu organizations undertook activities to mobilize public opinion for the construction of a Ram temple at the disputed site.

The Hindu idols continued to be housed inside the disputed structure after 1949. Hindus also continued to worship these idols without interruption. In 1984, the Vishwa Hindu Parishad (VHP) constituted a group to continue the movement and BJP leader L.K. Advani was put in charge of the campaign. The VHP organized a massive procession from Sitamarhi, which is believed to be the place where Lord Rama's wife Sita entered into the earth, to Ayodhya in late September 1984. The procession reached Ayodhya after twelve days.

The controversy remained at a low ebb till 1986 when the district court of Faizabad ordered the opening of the gates for Hindus, allowing them darshan and to hold puja before the idols in the sanctum sanctorum of the shrine. He also ordered the removal of all barriers, locks and the brick-and-iron grill wall as it created an artificial barrier between the idols and the devotees, but the inner courtyard continued to stay locked. Soon after this decision, the Babri Masjid Action Committee (BMAC) was constituted. The BMAC sought the restoration of the disputed shrine to the Muslims and launched a protest movement. The Hindu organizations, on the other hand, stepped up their activities to mobilize public opinion further.

The clamour for building a Ram temple was growing. It was during the late prime minister Rajiv Gandhi's tenure in 1989 that the VHP was allowed to lay the foundation stone (in a *shilanyas* or inaugural ceremony) of a Ram temple on an undisputed land close to the disputed mosque. Soon a fresh suit was filed by former VHP vice president Deoki Nandan Agarwala, as the next friend of Lord Rama, for declaration of the title and possession in its favour before the Lucknow bench of the Allahabad High Court. All the four suits pending before a Faizabad court were also transferred to the special bench of the high court. One of the cases filed by Nirmohi Akhara stated that for a long time in Ayodhya an ancient muth and akhara of Ramanandi Bairagis called Nirmohis existed and the Janmasthan, commonly known as Janmabhoomi, the birthplace of Lord Rama, belonged to it; the case also held that the akhara had always received and managed the offerings made in the form of money, etc., there. It was claimed that the Asthan of the Janmabhoomi was of great antiquity. The suit was confined to the inner courtyard and the constructed portion. The prayer in the suit was that the Nirmohi Akhara should be given possession of the temple.

L.K. Advani launched a cross-country rathyatra (pilgrimage procession) on 25 September 1990 from Somnath to Ayodhya to garner support for the move to build a Ram temple at the site. In November 1990, his rath was stopped at Samastipur, Bihar, where he was arrested.[2]

Displeased with his arrest, the BJP withdrew its support to the V.P. Singh government. The move triggered fresh elections. The BJP became India's primary opposition party in the Parliament and came to power in Uttar Pradesh in 1991.

The movement for building a temple gathered further momentum with kar sevaks pouring into Ayodhya. The BJP also declared its commitment to the construction of the temple. A plea was made to the Supreme Court to hold a *kar seva,* a symbolic gathering of kar sevaks. Based on the undertaking that no damage would be caused to the disputed structure, the kar seva was allowed. This led to the demolition of the Babri Masjid on 6 December 1992 and also resulted in communal unrest and riots.

The volatile situation made the P.V. Narasimha Rao–led Congress government at the Centre acquire a large area of about 68 acres, including the disputed premises, through the Acquisition of Certain Area at Ayodhya Act, 1993. Simultaneously, reference was also made by the President of India to the Supreme Court under Article 143 of the Constitution to decide 'whether a Hindu temple or any Hindu religious structure existed prior to the construction of the Ram Janam Bhoomi and Babri Masjid (including the premises of the inner and outer courtyards on such structure) in the area on which the structure stands or not'.

However, the five-judge bench of the Supreme Court refused to answer the reference in its 1994 judgment in the case, *Dr. M. Ismail Farooqi v. Union of India.* The Acquisition of Certain Area at Ayodhya Act, 1993, was also struck down as being unconstitutional. While reviving all the pending suits and partly upholding the validity of the Act, the top court appointed the Central government as the statutory receiver to manage the disputed area (inner and outer courtyard). It further held that the duty of the Central government as the statutory receiver would be to hand over the disputed area as per the final decision of the court. It was also clarified that the disputed area alone remained the subject matter of the revived suits and that the claim of Muslims over adjoining alleged graveyard was not left open to be decided.

Mumbai Riots

The destruction of the Babri Masjid in Ayodhya triggered some of the worst inter-communal violence since the Partition in 1947. The violence sent shockwaves throughout the country. More than 2000 people died in the riots throughout India.

The Cabinet met in an emergency session to dismiss the BJP-led government in Uttar Pradesh for failing to protect the mosque. Prime Minister Narasimha Rao repeatedly appealed for calm in radio and television broadcasts. 'What happened today is a matter of great concern and shame for all Indians,' he said.

BJP leader L.K. Advani also resigned as the leader of the Opposition, accepting 'moral responsibility' for the violence. He described the incident as 'very unfortunate', and said that he had appealed to the crowd still at the Babri Masjid site to leave.

The resolve of the VHP along with the BJP and the Rashtriya Swayamsevak Sangh (RSS) to build a temple at the disputed site was the root cause of the countrywide rioting.

After the demolition, Mumbai was the worst affected city. The 1993 Mumbai serial blasts, coordinated by underworld don Dawood Ibrahim, were carried out to avenge the demolition of the Babri Masjid. The financial capital witnessed twelve serial bomb explosions on 12 March 1993 which claimed about 257 lives and injured over 713 people.

Even after the 1993 blasts, the two communities were all set to settle scores under the garb of the Babri Masjid demolition. Almost ten years later, on 27 February 2002, a Muslim mob in the town of Godhra attacked and set fire to two carriages of the Sabarmati Express carrying Hindu activists. Fifty-eight people were killed, many of them women and children. The activists were returning from Ayodhya, where they had gone to support a VHP campaign to construct a temple.

This was followed by a three-day retaliatory killing spree, from 28 February to 2 March 2002, by Hindus, which left hundreds dead and tens of thousands homeless. The looting and burning of Muslim homes, shops, restaurants and places of worship was also widespread.

The Gujarat government chose to characterize the violence as a 'spontaneous reaction' to the incidents in Godhra. However, several human rights organizations felt that it was a planned attack. It is believed that the attacks on Muslims were part of a concerted campaign by Hindu nationalist organizations to promote and exploit communal tensions to further the BJP's political rule. The violence in Gujarat has triggered widespread outrage in India. Protests also erupted in Islamic nations. As anti-Hindu riots raged in Pakistan and Bangladesh, bitter criticism came from Turkey and Iran.

The High Court Judgment and Findings

On 30 September 2010, sixty years after the matter first went into litigation, the Lucknow bench of the Allahabad High Court ruled for a three-way division of the disputed area between the Sunni Waqf Board, the Nirmohi Akhara and the 'Ram Lalla' (infant Lord Rama), represented by the Hindu Mahasabha.

Two-thirds of the site is to be shared by the two Hindu plaintiffs and one-third will be given to the Sunni Waqf Board. By a 2:1 majority verdict, plaintiffs representing Lord Rama, the Nirmohi Akhara and the Sunni Waqf Board were declared joint title-holders of the property. The judgment asserted that the portion under the central dome of the demolished three-dome structure where the idol of Ram Lalla had been kept in a makeshift temple was the birthplace of Lord Rama, 'as per faith and belief of the Hindus', and was allotted to Hindus; the Nirmohi Akhara was given land including the Ram Chabutra and Sita Ki Rasoi.

The three-judge bench comprising justices S.U. Khan, Sudhir Agarwal and D.V. Sharma dismissed the petition filed by the Sunni Waqf Board for possession of the Babri Masjid because it was time-barred. It cited faith as the basis to declare the site the Janmasthan of Lord Rama, but ordered a three-way partition considering the historical use of the site by Muslims and Hindus. The bench further clarified that even though all the three parties are declared to have a one-third share each in the property, minor adjustments could be made—for which the adversely affected party would be compensated with a part of the adjoining land acquired by the Central government.

Justice Sharma, however, disagreed with the one-third formula. According to him, the outer courtyard was in the exclusive possession of Hindus for worship, and 'they were also worshipping' in the inner courtyard (of the disputed structure); hence, he held, Hindus had exclusive rights to the entire site. In his dissenting judgment, Justice Sharma categorically stated that 'the disputed site is the birthplace of Lord Ram'. He used the following rationale to support this:

[The] place of birth, that is Ram Janmabhumi, is a juristic person. The deity also attained divinity like Agni, Vayu, Kedarnath. Asthan is personified as the spirit of divine worshipped as the birthplace of Ram Lala or Lord Ram as a child. Spirit of divine ever remains present everywhere at all times for anyone to invoke [as] any shape or form in accordance with his own aspirations and it can be shapeless and formless also.

In effect, the ruling meant that Ram Lalla, being a deity, enjoyed all legal rights. 'In the Indian judicial system, deities have always been regarded as legal entities who can fight their case through the trustees or managing board in charge of the temple in which they are worshipped' by devotees.[3] While both judges—justices Agarwal and Sharma—said the mosque was built after the demolition of a Hindu temple, Justice Khan disagreed, saying that 'the mosque was constructed over ... temples which were lying in utter ruins [for] a very long time before the construction of the mosque and some material thereof was used in the construction of the mosque'.

However, Justice Agarwal and Justice Khan agreed that the building that existed until 1992 was a mosque. Justice Sharma disagreed: 'The disputed building was constructed by Babar ... against the tenets of Islam. Thus, it cannot have the character of a mosque.'

Justice Khan also noted that 'for some decades before 1949 Hindus started treating/believing the place beneath the central dome of the mosque to be the exact birthplace of Lord Ram'. However, he ordered that the portion below the central dome 'be allotted to Hindus in final decree'.

The HC also took into consideration a 2003 report by the Archaeological Survey of India that claimed to have found the ruins of a tenth-century temple beneath the site of the Babri Masjid, even though Muslim groups disputed the findings.

All the three contesting groups termed the HC decision partly disappointing and moved the Supreme Court, hoping that peace and tranquillity would prevail in the country and the issue would not be taken to the streets. However, after the HC judgment, people across the country spoke in one voice on the need to maintain calm.

Prime Minister Manmohan Singh issued an appeal to people to 'maintain peace and tranquillity and to show respect for all religions and religious beliefs in the highest traditions of Indian culture'. He further said, 'Let me also state that government on its part remains fully committed to upholding the rule of law and maintaining peace, order and harmony . . . It is my hope that the response of the people of India to the judgement will be respectful, dignified and do our country proud.'[4]

Welcoming the decision, Advani too issued a statement on behalf of his party:

In so far as the judgement upholds the right of the Hindus to construct a temple, it is a significant step forward towards the construction of a grand temple of the birthplace of Lord Ram . . . the BJP believes this verdict opens a new chapter for national integration and a new era of inter-community relations. The BJP is gratified that the nation has received the verdict with maturity.[5]

As per RSS chief Mohan Bhagwat:

[The] judgement has paved the way for the construction of the Ram temple in Ayodhya. The judgement is not a win or loss for anybody. We invite everybody, including Muslims, to help build the temple . . . joy and happiness over the verdict should find expression in a controlled and peaceful manner within the limits of law and constitution . . . the movement for a Ram temple was not a reactionary one, nor is it against any particular community.[6]

The Congress too welcomed the Ayodhya judgment, saying that everyone should accept it and no one should treat it as a victory or defeat. 'Congress has held that the controversy should either be solved through talks or the verdict of the court should be accepted,' the party's general secretary Janardan Dwivedi said.

The then Gujarat chief minister Narendra Modi said: 'We should all work towards harmony. I am happy that the judgement now paves the way for building a Ram temple in Ayodhya. This judgement will work as a catalyst for the country's unity.'

Zafaryab Jilani, convenor of the All-India Babri Masjid Action Committee (AIBMAC), too said, 'We hope peace and tranquility will be maintained.' He further added that the 'majority judgment is that mosque and temple must coexist'.

The Liberhan Commission

On 16 December 1992, ten days after the demolition, the Congress government at the Centre set up a commission of inquiry under Justice Liberhan. After almost seventeen years, on 30 June 2009, the commission submitted its report to the then prime minister Manmohan Singh. While its contents were not made public then, later it emerged that the report held sixty-eight people culpable, including top BJP leaders L.K. Advani, Dr Murli Manohar Joshi, former prime minister Atal Bihari Vajpayee, and former UP chief minister Kalyan Singh during whose regime the Babri Masjid was demolished.[7]

'Kalyan Singh, his ministers and his hand-picked bureaucrats created man-made and cataclysmic circumstances which could result in no consequences other than the demolition of the disputed structure . . . They denuded the

State of every legal, moral and statutory restraint and wilfully enabled and facilitated the wanton destruction and the ensuing anarchy,' the report stated.

In the 1000-page-long report, the commission also said that the demolition of the Babri Masjid was planned, systematic and was the outcome of communal intolerance deliberately created by the Sangh Parivar and its sister affiliates, including the BJP.

'It cannot be assumed even for a moment that Advani, Vajpayee or Joshi did not know the designs of the Sangh Parivar. Even though these leaders were deemed and used by the Parivar . . . to reassure the cautious masses, they were [in fact] party to the decisions which had been taken,' said Justice Liberhan, while recommending a law providing for exemplary punishment for misusing religion to acquire political power.

The Criminal Case

In the related criminal case, the Supreme Court on 19 April 2017 revived criminal conspiracy charges against twenty-one accused, including top BJP leaders L.K. Advani, Uma Bharti and Dr Murli Manohar Joshi, and held that the senior leaders will have to face trial in the Babri Masjid demolition case. Besides these three, the other accused leaders in the case include Giriraj Kishore, Vishnu Hari Dalmia, Vinay Katiyar and Sadvi Ritambara. Eight of the other accused have died so far.

The apex court also ordered a joint trial against the leaders and kar sevaks in Lucknow and directed that the day-to-day trial with the proceedings should be completed in two years. Kalyan Singh, who was the chief minister of Uttar Pradesh when the mosque was demolished, is currently the governor of Rajasthan and cannot be prosecuted while in office. His trial will begin after his term ends, the Supreme Court said.

Right after the demolition in December 1992, two set of cases were filed. The first case was filed against Advani and twelve others who were on the dais at Ram Katha Kunj in Ayodhya when the mosque was demolished. The FIR specifically charged Advani and other leaders with making inflammatory speeches and conspiracy to demolish the structure. The second was against unknown kar sevaks who were in and around the disputed structure during the demolition. While the trial against senior leaders was being held in Raebareli, a Lucknow court had started hearing cases against the kar sevaks.

The two cases investigated by the Uttar Pradesh Police were later merged and handed over to the CBI, which filed a composite charge sheet on 5 October 1993. The various charges that the CBI pressed against these accused include spreading communal frenzy, rioting, committing a criminal act with a common object, and creating ill will among different classes at a place of worship. The charge of criminal conspiracy, if added under Section 120(B) of the IPC, will make each of the accused responsible for the demolition, even if they were not directly involved in the act.

On 4 May 2001, the sessions judge had dropped the conspiracy charges against the BJP stalwarts on the grounds that the case related only to the kar sevaks. This order was also upheld by the Allahabad High Court, which ordered the dropping of conspiracy charges against twenty-one persons, including BJP leaders. The CBI then moved the Supreme Court to try the accused political leaders. The agency stated that it had evidence that the BJP leaders, who had made their speeches on a stage near the mosque on the day that it was razed to the ground, were part of the deadly plan to bring down the mosque. The clubbing of the two cases in Lucknow was earlier opposed by the lawyers representing Advani and Joshi on the grounds that they involve different people as the accused.

After the Supreme Court judgment asked the BJP leaders to join the trial, the Union water resources minister Uma Bharti said she was ready to sacrifice her life for the construction of the Ram temple. 'Grand Ram temple in Ayodhya is my dream. Ready to go to prison or be hanged for India and Ram Mandir,' she said, adding that she was 'proud and unapologetic', that she did not repent her role in the Ram Janmabhoomi campaign and was ready to face whatever punishment came her way.[8]

Supreme Court Proceedings

The Supreme Court three-judge bench, headed by Chief Justice Dipak Misra, has fixed 5 December 2017—the eve of the twenty-fifth anniversary of the demolition—for hearing cross-appeals against the September 2010 judgment of the Allahabad High Court, which divided the 2.77 acres of disputed land between the deity Ram Lalla, the Sunni Waqf Board and the Nirmohi Akhara.

All the appeals against the division of the property as

ordered by the high court were stayed by the Supreme Court in 2011. In March 2017, the apex court had suggested that the dispute must be settled amicably through 'a cordial meeting' of all parties; the former chief justice J.S. Khehar had offered to personally mediate the issue.

BJP leader Subramanian Swamy has also joined the case recently, seeking permission to build a Ram temple at the site of the demolished Babri Masjid. Though he was not a party to the main appeals, he claimed that 'my right to pray is affected by the pending case'.

Jilani, convenor of the AIBMAC, has termed the high court judgment as 'faulty' and not in accordance with the law and evidence supplied by Muslims to establish that they had remained in exclusive possession of the inner portion of the mosque up to 22 December 1949. According to him:

It is absolutely false to suggest that Babur had ever demolished any temple at Ayodhya. The established historical fact is that Babar had never entered Ayodhya. It was his Commander Meer Baqi who had built the Mosque and had dedicated it to Babur. Had any Ram temple been demolished in 1528, the same must have been mentioned in history books ... demolition of Somnath Temple about 500 years prior to 1528 finds detailed mention in these books. It is thus obvious that no temple was demolished in or around 1528 at Ayodhya, much less any Ram temple on the so-called place of birth of Lord Rama.

The Ayodhya case has been a game changer in the political history of the country. The issue is intrinsically entwined with power politics, with each party trying to exploit it to suit their own agenda and political motives. In 1991, the BJP gained heavily in popularity as the party advocating the building of the Ram temple. Though the BJP government had to resign after the demolition, the incident became a turning point in the Indian polity, especially for parties trying to get a foothold in politics. Several political groups also emerged, leading to the aggressive growth of caste identity politics in the country. It also led to the emergence of the BJP at the national level. Former solicitor general of India and senior lawyer Mohan Parasaran said:

> Justice though delayed, is not denied in this case. The proceedings will be taken to their logical end as directed by the Supreme Court. Whatever be the ultimate judicial outcome, I would rate this incident as highly influential in shaping the legal and political history of the county, leading to resurgence of Hindu religious forces and the consolidation of the BJP.

Having said that, no contesting party wants to lose its grip over the disputed site. Leaders of the BMAC and the Muslim Personal Law Board have declared that they are not prepared for any compromise on their plans to rebuild the mosque at the disputed site. As per Jilani:

> It is most unjust to say that flagrant violation of the rights of Muslims in respect of a Historical Mosque should be

ignored in the name of so called 'peace in the region'. It is a
matter of rule of law and constitutional guarantees given in
Articles 25 and 26 of the Constitution of India.

Right-wing parties also want the construction of the
temple to be started soon at the disputed site. In view of the
widening gap between the two communities, the former chief
justice of India had asked the conflicting parties to reach an
out-of-court settlement to resolve the issue. It is felt that any
further contest would invariably result in causing bitterness
and frustration and will be detrimental to the cause of much-
needed peace and inter-religious harmony in the region.

Though the idea of resolving the dispute through
negotiations is not entirely new, it is imperative that concerted
efforts are made by all peace-loving people of the country
to find an amicable solution to the problem. Now all eyes
are set on how the Supreme Court will resolve the 500-odd
year dispute.

In conclusion, it is worth mentioning Allahabad HC judge
Justice Khan's epilogue in his judgment:

Muslims must also ponder that at present the entire world
wants to know the exact teaching of Islam in respect [to]
relationship of Muslims with others. Hostility—peace—
friendship—tolerance—opportunity to impress others with
the Message—opportunity to strike wherever and whenever
possible—or what? In this regard Muslims in India enjoy a
unique position. They have been rulers here, they have been
ruled and now they are sharers in power (of course junior
partners). They are not in majority but they are also not

negligible minority ([the] maximum member of Muslims in any country after Indonesia is in India). In other countries either the Muslims are in huge majority which makes them indifferent to the problem in question or in negligible minority which makes them redundant. Indian Muslims have also inherited huge legacy of religious learning and knowledge. They are therefore in the best position to tell the world the correct position. Let them start with their role in the resolution of the conflict at hand.

5

'None of the Above'

The Choice to Not Choose

'Two roads diverged in a wood, and I—
I took the one less traveled by,
And that has made all the difference.'

—Robert Frost

It's a matter of choice, our decision, that makes all the difference.

'None of the above' or NOTA is a ballot option that voters choose to convey that no candidate from their constituency is worthy of their votes in the elections.

NOTA was introduced in India following the 2013 Supreme Court judgment in the *People's Union for Civil Liberties v. Union of India* case. Thus, India entered the league of thirteen countries that have instituted negative voting and acknowledged that the right to reject candidates in elections is a part of the fundamental right to freedom of speech and expression. These countries—which include

France, Belgium, Brazil, Greece, Ukraine, Chile, Bangladesh, Finland, Sweden, United States of America, Colombia and Spain—have provided for neutral/protest/negative voting in their electoral systems.

The option was introduced to enable those members of the electorate who do not wish to vote for any of the candidates to exercise their right without having the secrecy of their decision violated.

When the Supreme Court delivered this historic judgment in 2013, the NOTA option already existed, but with certain riders. Under the previous version of the option, as per Rule 49-O of the Conduct of Election Rules, 1961, in order to cast a negative ballot a voter had to inform the presiding officer at the polling booth. Before the full-fledged NOTA option came into existence, people casting negative votes were required to enter their names in a register and record their vote on a separate paper ballot. This would compromise the secrecy of the candidates.

The inclusion of the NOTA button on Electronic Voting Machines (EVMs) ensures that the right to vote and the right not to vote stand on the same pedestal and that the secrecy of the voting process is maintained. The NOTA option is at the end of the candidate list on the EVMs.

NOTA, as of now, is just a symbolic step to strengthen the democratic set-up of India. It, however, does not grant the right to reject a candidate. The candidate with the maximum votes still wins the election, irrespective of the number of NOTA votes polled. Though NOTA is electronically counted, it does not affect the election results. Even if the NOTA votes exceed 50 per cent of the total votes cast, the winner is selected on the basis of the rest of the votes, in keeping with the first-past-the-post system.

As per the provisions of Clause(A) of Rule 64 of the Conduct of Election Rules, 1961, read with Section 65 of the Representation of the People Act (RPA), 1951, the candidate who has polled the largest number of valid votes is to be declared elected by the returning officer. Even if a candidate gets just one vote out of a total of 10,000 votes, and the rest of the 9999 voters have opted for the NOTA option, the candidate will be declared elected.

Founded by veteran leader Jaya Prakash Narayan in 1976, the People's Union for Civil Liberties and Democratic Rights—later renamed as the People's Union for Civil Liberties (PUCL)—is an NGO that seeks to introduce reforms in the electoral system. In 2002, PUCL filed a public interest litigation (PIL) with the Supreme Court, seeking the grant of the right to reject candidates in elections. Questioning the constitutional validity of the existing rules,[1] the PIL alleged that the then existing provisions violated the secrecy of voting, which is fundamental to free and fair elections and is required to be maintained as per Section 128 of the RPA, 1951, and Rules 39 and 49-M.

PUCL, represented by senior lawyer Rajinder Sachar, argued that though the rules recognized the right of a voter not to vote, the secrecy over not voting was not maintained. Thus, the impugned rules were also violative of Articles 19(1)(a) and 21 of the Constitution of India, besides international covenants. PUCL sought that the two rules in question be declared ultra vires and unconstitutional. Sachar asked the Election Commission of India to provide necessary provision in the ballot papers as well as in the EVMs for the protection of the right not to vote.

However, in February 2009, a division bench of the Supreme Court referred the PIL to a larger bench after various objections were raised on its maintainability. One of the arguments submitted by Additional Solicitor General P.P. Malhotra was on the grounds that the right to vote is neither a fundamental right nor a constitutional right nor a common law right. It is a pure and simple statutory right as enshrined in Part III of the Constitution, a view that was taken by the apex court in its earlier judgments.

Fundamental rights are protected and guaranteed by the Constitution and cannot be taken away by an ordinary law enacted by the legislature. If a fundamental right is violated, the Constitution provides that the affected person may move to the high court or Supreme Court. On the other hand, statutory rights may be limited or extinguished by an amendment or repeal and are subordinate to the higher constitutional laws.

Malhotra asserted that neither the RPA nor the Constitution declared the right to vote as anything more than a statutory right and hence the PIL should be dismissed. The law officer further pointed out that the right of secrecy has been extended to only those voters who have exercised their right to vote and the same, in no manner, can be extended to those who have not voted at all. Finally, he submitted that since Section 2(d) of the RPA specifically defines 'election' to mean an election to fill a seat, it cannot be construed as an election not to fill a seat.

He asserted that elections gave voters the choice to pick

their representative from among various candidates with the objective to fill a seat. He concluded that negative voting (NOTA) had no legal consequence and that there would be no motivation for voters to travel to the polling booth and reject all the candidates, which would have the same effect as not going to the polling station at all.

Counsel Meenakshi Arora, appearing for the Election Commission of India, had argued that secrecy was an essential feature of 'free and fair elections' and that the existing rules violated the requirement of secrecy.

She said that the Election Commission had sent a letter to the Secretary, Ministry of Law and Justice, on 10 December 2001,which pointed out that the electoral right under the relevant law[2] includes the right not to cast vote and sought to provide a panel in the EVMs so that an elector may indicate that he or she does not wish to vote for any of the contesting candidates. The letter also stated that such number of votes expressing dissatisfaction with all the candidates may be recorded in a result sheet. However, the government was not in favour of such an idea.

Arora also agreed that in the larger interest of promoting democracy, a provision for the NOTA button should be made in the EVMs and ballot papers. This was to ensure that such an action, apart from promoting free and fair elections in a democracy, will provide an opportunity to the elector to express his dissent/disapproval against the contesting candidates and will have the benefit of reducing bogus voting.

Counsel Kamini Jaiswal and Raghenth Basant, on behalf of the intervener, also supported the inclusion of NOTA in EVMs so that the voters who come to the polling booth could exercise the right not to vote without compromising on their right to secrecy during the voting process.

The NOTA Verdict

With a view to bring 'purity' in elections, the Supreme Court in a landmark judgment on 27 September 2013 allowed voters to cast negative votes and reject all candidates as unworthy of being elected. The voter could press the NOTA button on the EVM, it said, directing the Election Commission to provide this option on EVMs and ballot papers in a phased manner and also asked the Centre to give its support to make this happen.

The apex court said that the right to vote and the right to say 'none of the above' both constitute a basic right of the voters. 'When a large number of voters will press NOTA button, it will force political parties to choose better candidates. Negative voting would lead to systemic change in polls,' it said, observing that the implementation of the option was akin to the 'abstain' option given to MPs and MLAs during voting in the Parliament and state assemblies. If the right to vote is a statutory right, then the right to reject candidates is a fundamental right to speech and expression under the Constitution, it held.

'For democracy to survive, it is essential that the best available men should be chosen ... for proper governance of the country. This can be best achieved through men of high moral and ethical values who win the elections on a positive vote,' said a bench comprising Chief Justice of India (CJI) P. Sathasivam and justices Ranjana Desai and Ranjan Gogoi.

In the written judgment, the CJI said: 'Giving right to a voter not to vote for any candidate while protecting his right of secrecy is extremely important in a democracy.' In a fifty-page judgment, the bench stated that negative voting would foster purity and vibrancy of elections and ensure wide participation as people who are unsatisfied with the candidates in the fray would also turn up to express their opinion, rejecting unscrupulous elements and impersonators. The right to reject candidates in elections is a part of the fundamental right to freedom of speech and expression granted by the Constitution to Indian citizens; democracy is all about choice, and the significance of the right of citizens to cast negative voting is massive, it said. It said that the secrecy of votes cast under the NOTA option must be maintained by the Election Commission. However, the judgment did not delve into a situation where the votes cast under this option outnumber the votes received by the candidates. The path-breaking verdict was part of a series of judgments (including the Lily Thomas judgment detailed in Chapter 8) passed by the apex court to instate electoral reforms, meant to further empower the voters in exercising their franchise and help cleanse the political system of the country.

For the first time, the principle of the right to reject was recognized. A quality change in the boisterous Indian elections was brought in. The ballot paper now has the option of 'none of the above' or in general parlance NOTA. It was first introduced in the general elections of 2014 and subsequently in the assembly elections. The idea was to strengthen the democracy further.

Significantly, the judgment gave dignity to the right to vote. By declaring that the right to vote is essentially a right to free expression, the judgment brought this under the purview of fundamental rights. The court recognized that the right to vote included the right not to vote, thereby underlining equal opportunity for all.

Senior Supreme Court advocate Dr Abhishek Singhvi, MP, former chairman, Parliamentary Standing Committee on Law and Justice, and national spokesperson, Congress, said:

> The court also pressed into service two less complicated principles. One was the need to operationalize freedom of expression and its manifestation, which would otherwise be violated in the absence of NOTA. Secondly, the court noted that within Parliament and all state legislatures, there is the option not only for the binary 'yes' and 'no' but also a specific option to press the abstain button. A similar option, the court said, must be given to the voter who elects such legislators, if the latter have this option within legislatures! Interestingly, the court not only held the absence of such an option to be unconstitutional but affirmatively directed its specific inclusion in the balloting system.

Talking of its larger implication, senior advocate Mohan Parasaran, who is a former solicitor general of India, said:

> This judgment is perhaps another stepping stone towards the development of democracy and the democratic process

in India. The option of exercising the vote for NOTA is available in a few countries. Fielding candidates in an election has always been subject to party politics, nepotism and the whims of those who are in power, as a result of which deserving candidates tend to lose out. This resulted in the voter being forced to vote for a candidate as a matter of last resort rather than as a matter of first choice.

A vibrant democracy gives voters an opportunity to press the NOTA button. This option was expected to force political parties to nominate the best candidates. One may point out that this has not significantly altered the situation as candidates with criminal antecedents continue to be elected. But the NOTA option in the long run will, to a great extent, help weed out the unwanted.

The then Gujarat chief minister Narendra Modi, who is now the prime minister, and veteran BJP leader L.K. Advani had welcomed the NOTA provision then. They had also asked for another electoral reform—to make voting mandatory.

'I hold, therefore, that a negative vote would become really meaningful if it is accompanied also by the introduction of mandatory voting,' Advani wrote in a blog.[3]

The NOTA option was first used in the 2013 assembly elections held in four states—Chhattisgarh, Mizoram, Rajasthan and Madhya Pradesh and the former Union Territory, Delhi. More than 15 lakh people exercised the option in the state polls. Around 50,000 voters opted for NOTA in Delhi; 3.56 lakh in Chhattisgarh; 5.9 lakh in Madhya Pradesh; and 5.67 lakh in Rajasthan.[4]

The number of voters who pressed the NOTA button in

the Uttar Pradesh assembly elections held in March 2017 was unprecedented and an indicator of the lack of faith in and anger against the political parties and their candidates. In twelve constituencies of the state, 7,57,643 votes were polled. NOTA accounted for about 0.9 per cent of the total votes polled. In each of these rural constituencies, the NOTA poll was bigger than the margin of victory.

In the assembly constituency of Domariyaganj, the victory margin was only 171 votes, while NOTA polled 1611 votes. The Mohanlalganj constituency recorded a victory margin of only 530 votes and the NOTA poll was 3471. Likewise in Dudhi, NOTA polled 8522 votes while the victory margin between the winner and runner-up was only 1085 votes. The victory margin in the Mant assembly constituency was 432 votes, while NOTA polled 1253 votes, which was almost three times the victory margin. In Matera too, the NOTA poll was 2717 votes and the margin of victory was only 1595 votes. In the Meerapur constituency, the victory margin was only 193 votes and NOTA polled 1090 votes. In Mubarakpur, NOTA polled 1628 votes and the margin of victory was only 688 votes.[5]

Therefore, it can be affirmed that the NOTA option will play a crucial role in forcing political parties to shun candidates with criminal or immoral backgrounds. The very intent of introducing this option is empowering the voter to reject all candidates if they do not like any of them. The political parties would be left with no option other than to field clean candidates.

Consider these events. In Kerala, a group of women activists hit the road urging people not to elect any candidate if no woman was present in the fray. In Tamil Nadu, a youth group campaigned for NOTA as a protest vote against corruption. One doesn't need more proof of voter empowerment.

In absolute numbers, NOTA polling is small. On an average, the maximum NOTA vote share has not crossed 2.02 per cent of the total votes polled in an election. The early trends of the NOTA polls need to be explored further with more elaborate analysis. This electoral option will become a significant means of negative voting only if it is exercised as the 'right to reject' rather than serving as a symbolic instrument to express resentment.

Some political experts hold the view that the NOTA option is essentially a waste of a vote since it makes no impact in the electoral outcome in any election. They say that since it is merely cosmetic in nature, it can only work when coupled with the 'right to recall' option. The right to recall is one of the facets of direct democracy that refers to a process whereby an electorate is able to recall an elected representative for underperformance, corruption or mismanagement while still in office, by filing a petition that triggers a re-election, usually after a particular percentage of people sign the petition. The said political experts believe that granting the electorate the right to recall will instil fear in candidates to do well in office. In addition, it will act as a signifier of public displeasure.

The demand for the right to recall gained momentum when in 2011 reformists such as Anna Hazare made a strong case for it. The practice of the right to recall (also called the 'recall referendum' or 'representative recall') exists in Switzerland, the United States, the United Kingdom, Canada and Venezuela. Hazare, too, felt that the grant of such a right would curb corruption and enable voters to reject an incompetent person. By providing a tool to dissatisfied citizens to rectify their mistake, the right to recall could help deter underperformance, mismanagement, corruption and apathy on the candidate's part.

But the demand was rejected by other political analysts, who felt that the recall is fraught with serious consequences and would only add to the instability of governments by empowering not those who win elections but those who lose. The latter can, in theory, bring about a recall at the drop of a hat. They felt that the elected representatives would be under constant pressure to work the way people want them to and deter them from taking strong decisions.

At present, the right to recall option is prescribed for local elections in Chhattisgarh, Madhya Pradesh, Rajasthan and Maharashtra and there are demands for introducing this system at the state and parliamentary level. However, its proponents have not detailed the governing procedural framework, namely the percentage of electors needed to sign the petition; the grounds for initiating a recall, or whether any grounds are necessary; or the minimum period, if any, after which a recall can be initiated. Neither have they specified which authority would be competent to decide whether the recall may be commenced, based on the satisfaction of certain preconditions.

The Law Commission of India in its 255th report on Electoral Reforms rejected both the right to reject and right to recall options. 'The Law Commission currently rejects the extension of the NOTA principle to introduce a right to reject the candidate and invalidate the election in cases where a majority of the votes have been polled in favour of the NOTA option. However, the issue might be reconsidered again in the future.'

The Association for Democratic Reforms and the National Election Watch have recommended that votes cast for the NOTA option should also be counted in a particular constituency. In case the NOTA option gets more votes than any of the candidates, none of the candidates should be declared elected and a fresh election should be held in which none of the candidates from the previous election are allowed to recontest.

This may appear to be a cumbersome and tedious process but it will nudge the entire system in the direction of better representativeness among the elected candidates by reducing the sectarian effects of vote banks. It will also encourage political parties to put up better candidates.

Elections are held in the country to elect the right person—a person who has high ethical and moral values and who may work for the upliftment of the country. This is possible only when they are held in a free, fair and transparent manner.

There is a category of voters who never go to vote or don't care for the elections as they think that no candidate is up to their expectations. The NOTA option will definitely motivate them to exercise their franchise in total secrecy. This could accelerate effective participation among empowered voters.

When instating the NOTA option, the Supreme Court opined that this move will not bring change at once, but will gradually help replace corrupt candidates in the election process with people who have a clean image. It will also make the elections more transparent.

Technically, both the right to reject and right to recall are designed to achieve the same objective. The former would allow voters to reject candidates with criminal or otherwise tainted backgrounds. The right to reject may not serve the democracy in practice yet, but in principle it is a game changer. The provision of casting a negative vote would be a powerful tool indeed, especially if it could be enabled against each individual candidate. This way, criminals who want to extend their influence into politics could be uprooted. Also, politicians who do not serve well, are corrupt and/or underperformers will be made accountable to the public on judgement (election) day.

6

The Uphaar Tragedy

Trial by Fire

'It has been said that time heals all wounds. I don't agree. The wounds remain. Time—the mind, protecting its sanity—covers them with some scar tissue and the pain lessens, but it is never gone.'

—Rose Kennedy

A thick column of smoke billowed and engulfed the Uphaar Cinema complex in south Delhi. It was a gruesome spectacle. Recalling the threatening fire, Vinod Kumar Gupta, a tea vendor, said:

I heard screams from the back gate and rushed there . . . I saw someone throw a child down the first floor. I was so dumbstruck I couldn't rush to catch him. I don't know what happened to him but that sight pushed me to act. A crowd had gathered and we fetched mattresses from Uphaar Mattress Shop and laid them below the windows for those who jumped. I must have called the fire brigade and the police six, seven times.[1]

It was the fateful day of 13 June 1997. *Border*, an Indian multi-starrer war film, had just been released. Produced and directed by J.P. Dutta, the film starring Sunny Deol, Sunil Shetty, Akshaye Khanna and Jackie Shroff in pivotal roles is inspired from real-life events that happened at the Battle of Longewala during the Indo-Pakistan War of 1971. It was the highest-grossing Bollywood film of the year 1997.

The star-studded film attracted everyone with its patriotic fervour. Soldiers in uniform, fighting and sacrificing their lives for the country—it was nothing short of heroic. Those were the days when the Internet was still nascent in India. War movies have always been a treat to watch on the big screen, perhaps because of the adrenaline rush they offer. Never before had the reel and the real merged together in such a grotesque fashion—as people perished on screen, so did the people watching the movie. So engrossed was the audience in this war film that when smoke began to fill the main auditorium, they thought it was a special-effects display. It was pitch-dark and soon the auditorium turned into a gas chamber. There was complete pandemonium inside the auditorium and balcony.

A spark in an electricity transformer on the ground floor of the cinema hall had caused the fire. It soon spread to the adjacent parking area, setting several cars ablaze. The toxic smoke entered the auditorium through the stairwell and air-conditioning ducts.

There were about 750 people on the first floor of the

cinema—they managed to flee. Those in the balcony were not so lucky. There were not enough exits, no emergency lights and no fire alarms. The projector operator was not given instructions to stop the film while the fire was raging. There were neither public announcements nor any cinema staff to guide them. The doors to the middle entrance of the balcony were found to be bolted by the gatekeeper who had left his post without handing over the charge to his reliever.

The balcony viewers included Unnati and her thirteen-year-old brother Ujjwal, who were excited to watch the matinee show on the first day of its release. They had premium seats in the 'A' row of the balcony, just three seats away from the gangway on the right. Unfortunately, the siblings, with many others, got trapped in the balcony. The toxic fumes inside the hall caused asphyxiation, killing fifty-nine people, out of which twenty-three were children, including Unnati and Ujjwal. Hundreds of people were injured in the ensuing stampede.

It took an hour to extinguish the fire. The people trapped in the balcony were rescued only once the bolted doors were opened; the damage to human life was irreparable. The poignant lyrics of a song from the film will always reverberate through the lives of those who lost their loved ones that day:

Sandeshay aate hain
Humein tadpaate hain
To chitthi aati hai
To poochh jaati hai
Ke ghar kab aaoge
Likho kab aaoge

Messages arrive
They torment us
Letters arrive
They keep on asking us
When will you come home
Write, when will you come

Sadly, many people never returned home that day. It was a black Friday. The management and employees of Uphaar Cinema were aware of the fact that a fire had broken out, but no one from the staff or management was present to lend a helping hand in the rescue operations.

The Uphaar Cinema tragedy was one of the worst nightmares for film lovers in India. The cinema hall was sealed after this horrifying tragedy.

Sheer negligence and greed were considered the main reasons behind the mishap, which claimed fifty-nine innocent lives. There were forty-three extra seats in the balcony and an eight-seater private box for the owners, the Ansals. This had completely blocked the exits on the right side of the balcony. These exits could have saved the lives of many people.

'Had the gangway not been blocked, my children—Unnati and Ujwal—would have walked to safety,' said their mother, Neelam Krishnamoorthy. 'I tried to convince them that we will watch the movie together after [a] few days. But they insisted, so I booked tickets for them. That is one decision I regret till date,' recalled the inconsolable mother. The parents of Unnati and Ujwal, Neelam Krishnamoorthy and Sekhar Krishnamoorthy, have been fighting the case from lower courts to the Supreme Court, for justice to the victims. The Krishnamoorthys have narrated the whole fire incident, as well as their trials and tribulations, in their book *Trial by Fire.*

Probe and Arrest

An FIR was filed at the Hauz Khas Police Station. The investigation into the incident was initially conducted by the Delhi Police. A month after the incident, in July 1997, Sushil Ansal and his son Pranav were arrested by the Delhi Police from Mumbai. Within two days of their arrest, the case was transferred to the Crime Branch and eventually to the Central Bureau of Investigation (CBI) on 25 July 1997.

The CBI soon sought various inspection-cum-scrutiny reports from the Central Building Research Institute, experts from the Public Works Department (PWD), the Municipal Corporation of Delhi (MCD), electricity department, and the Delhi Fire Service for structural and safety deviations. Forensic and post-mortem reports revealed that the cause of death was asphyxiation.

The probe was completed within a month of the tragedy; it held the owners of Uphaar Cinema—Sushil Ansal and his brother Gopal Ansal—the Delhi Vidyut Board (DVB), MCD, electricity department and the Delhi Fire Service responsible for the negligence.

It found that the authorities and the Ansal brothers had knowledge of the deviations from fire-safety norms, and despite that they had continued exhibiting films, thereby endangering the lives of all those who patronized the theatre. The CBI arraigned employees of the PWD, MCD and DVB as accused in the case and charged them with causing death due to negligence.

Trial by Fire

The charge sheet was filed against sixteen accused, including theatre owners Sushil Ansal and his brother Gopal Ansal in November 1997. Two years later, a sessions court headed by L.D. Malik started the trial. Charges were framed on 27 February 2001 under various sections, including Sections 304 (culpable homicide), 304-A (causing death by negligence) and 337 (causing hurt by act endangering life or personal safety of others) of the Indian Penal Code (IPC).

However, all the accused persons pleaded not guilty to the charges framed against them and wanted a trial. They moved the Delhi High Court against the order of framing charges; this appeal was dismissed. An appeal to the Supreme Court by Sushil Ansal was also rejected on 12 April 2002.

At the trial, 115 witnesses were examined in support of the case, and nearly 893 documents were scrutinized over the course of the proceedings. The eyewitnesses narrated the events and gave graphic accounts of the heart-wrenching incident. The evidence also comprised the depositions of relatives of some of the victims, including the Krishnamoorthys. Some of the onlookers and others who helped in the rescue operations were also examined by the prosecution, apart from the officers of the Delhi Fire Service and MCD.

Looking at the slow pace of the trial, the Delhi High Court rapped the lower court for tardiness, asking it to expedite the proceedings and wrap up the case by 15 December 2002. The case went on for another five years. On 20 November 2007, the trial court sentenced the Ansal brothers and ten others to a two-year imprisonment. It found that all the violations were committed while Sushil and Gopal were either directors or the managing directors of Ansal Theatre & Clubotels Pvt. Ltd, the company which ran the cinema hall. Even after the alleged resignation of the Ansal brothers in 1988, they continued to be in control of the management of the cinema and the running of its day-to-day affairs, including exercising control over the managers and other staff, the court stated.

The trial court further noted that the management had disregarded the requirements of law and the sanctioned plan, thereby putting the lives of the patrons at risk. This, according to the court, was gross negligence that had contributed to the death of a large number of people and had caused injuries to many more.

A year later, on 19 December 2008, the Delhi High Court also upheld the trial court's order convicting the Ansal brothers but reduced their sentence to a rigorous year-long imprisonment, without interfering with the fine imposed by the trial court. On 24 April 2003, the high court had directed the brothers to pay a compensation of Rs 18 crore to the relatives of the victims.

A year later, on 4 January 2008, the high court granted them bail along with two other accused but the Supreme Court cancelled it a few months later on 11 September and the Ansals were put behind bars.

On 30 January 2009, in an unusual move, the apex court again granted bail to Sushil and Gopal Ansal. Ram Jethmalani, former law minister and the country's top criminal lawyer, was instrumental in securing bail for his clients, the Ansal brothers.

On an earlier occasion, in 2005, Jethmalani had criticized Justice B.N. Agrawal in certain newspaper articles he had written. In a shrewd move, Jethmalani got the judge to quit the Uphaar case by recalling this criticism. The veteran lawyer told Justice Agrawal that he would feel awkward presenting the case of his clients before him. Soon after, a visibly anguished judge recused himself from hearing the Ansals' bail plea. Justice Agrawal had cancelled the Ansals' bail in September.

After his withdrawal, the matter was assigned to another bench consisting of justices S.B. Sinha and V.S. Sirpurkar and the Ansals got bail. Jethmalani wrote to the Supreme Court Registry that the matter should not be listed before the bench headed by Justice Agrawal.

'This is contempt of court,' the senior lawyer K.T.S. Tulsi had said, expressing his concern. However, Justice Sinha had brushed aside his objection by asking him to file a separate petition in this regard. Jethmalani's success had then led to many wondering if it marked the beginning of a trend that could have serious implications for the judicial administration system.

In 2011, the Supreme Court also fixed the civil liability of compensation for the case. It ordered Rs 10 lakh each for the next of kin of victims above twenty years of age, and Rs 7.5 lakh each for victims under twenty years. In October 2012, the Ansals made a futile attempt to end the fifteen-year-old criminal case by making an offer to pay for more damages, which was rejected by the victims of the Uphaar tragedy.

The Association of Victims of Uphaar Tragedy (AVUT), a body formed by victims' families, moved the Supreme Court for enhancement of the sentence and alteration of charges. The CBI too filed an appeal seeking enhancement and review of the verdict in 2009.

On 5 March 2014, a two-judge bench of justices T.S. Thakur and Gyan Sudha Misra of the Supreme Court upheld the conviction. However, considering their advanced age and the period already spent by them in prison, it decided not to send them back to jail and rather asked them to pay a fine of Rs 30 crore each in lieu of a jail term.

While both judges unanimously agreed that the Ansals had 'contemptuous disregard' for the law and affirmed their conviction, they differed on the quantum of sentence for Sushil, seventy-six, and Gopal, sixty-seven.

While Justice Thakur had retained the one-year jail term awarded by the high court in 2008, Justice Misra awarded the maximum punishment of two years to each brother, with the second year substituted with a fine of Rs 100 crore to be paid equally by the brothers. She also directed that in view of his advanced age, Sushil's jail term would be what he had already undergone. The fine amount was directed to be used for the construction of a trauma-care centre and super-speciality hospital in Delhi.

'The brothers were at the helm of affairs at the time of the tragedy and therefore they cannot escape the blame and pass it on to others, including the municipal or electricity authorities. They owed a duty of care to the people who went to the cinema,' said Justice Thakur, adding that the deaths had occurred mainly due to the inability of the victims to exit the cinema hall. Justice Misra agreed with the senior judge, holding the brothers guilty of 'gross criminal negligence'. So the question of the sentence was referred to a larger bench, following a split verdict.

Senior counsel Ram Jethmalani had argued that if the offence had been committed by the company, officers of the company could not be vicariously held guilty of criminal negligence. It was argued that in the absence of any provisions in the IPC rendering the officers of the company vicariously liable for prosecution for the offences committed by the company, there was no question of the Ansal brothers being held guilty, that too for an offence committed long after they had ceased to hold any position in the company.

Senior counsel Harish Salve and K.T.S. Tulsi, appearing for the CBI and the victims association, respectively, contended that while there was no quarrel with the proposition that death must be shown to have occurred as a direct, immediate or proximate result of an act of rashness or negligence, it was not correct to say that the deaths in this case had occurred because of the fire in the transformer.

Accepting their stand, Justice Thakur said:

One of the ingredients of an offence punishable under Section 304A of IPC indeed is that the rash or negligent act of the accused ought to be the direct, immediate and proximate cause of the death . . . The principle of law that death must be shown to be the direct, immediate and proximate result of the rash or negligent act is well accepted . . . It would in such circumstances make no difference whether the fire had started from a source within the cinema complex or outside, or whether the occupiers of the cinema were responsible for the fire or someone else.

. . . The important question to ask is what the immediate cause of the death was. If failure to exit was the immediate cause of death, nothing further need be considered. Smoke entered the cinema hall and the balcony and escape was prevented or at least delayed because of breach of the common law and statutory duty to care.

He also granted the accused three weeks' time to surrender. After this, on 19 August 2015, the three-judge bench of justices A.R. Dave, Kurian Joseph and Adarsh Kumar Goel enhanced the sentence to the maximum period of two years under Section 304-A (causing death by negligence) of the IPC if they failed to pay the fine amount of Rs 30 crore each within three months.

Justice Dave's bench had delivered its decision after the case was repeatedly adjourned over a period of seventeen months in the Supreme Court itself. The 2015 judgment issue was again reviewed on 9 February 2017. The Supreme Court, in a majority judgment of 2:1, decided to send Gopal Ansal back to jail for negligence and gave him four weeks to surrender, while sparing his elder brother Sushil from serving time behind bars due to his advanced age. Since Gopal had previously served four months and twenty days in jail, he was asked to serve the remainder of the sentence which was six months.

Subsequently, the bench came to be headed by Justice Ranjan Gogoi, owing to the retirement of Justice Dave. This bench said that the order of sentencing Gopal to one year in jail had to be 'maintained' without treating him on a par with his elder sibling. 'On principle of parity, the same benefit was extended to Gopal Ansal; but he never had a case of any age-related complications. Therefore, it is not a case to apply the principle of parity. To that extent, the order needs to be reviewed,' held the majority, while partly allowing the review petitions moved by the CBI and AVUT against the 2015 verdict.

The court also upheld its previous judgment directing the Ansals to pay a total compensation of Rs 60 crore, saying it was not 'excessive'. The third judge on the bench, Justice A.K. Goel, however, dissented and dismissed the need for a review of the previous verdict. The bench didn't feel the need to send Sushil Ansal back to jail. The fine amount was also directed to be utilized for the benefit of the public—the establishment of a trauma centre in the capital.

On 9 February 2017, seeking parity with his elder brother Sushil, Gopal made a last-ditch attempt to avoid serving the remainder of the one-year jail term. The Supreme Court rejected his appeal. His counsel Jethmalani sought pardon on 'humanitarian grounds'. He contended that Gopal's health had deteriorated and he was 'almost a dead person' and 'practically living on charity'. But his plea failed to impress Justice Ranjan Gogoi, who is next in line to become the Chief Justice of India. Even the AVUT's plea for review was rejected by the apex court.

After the verdict, senior lawyer Salman Khurshid, who appeared for the real-estate barons, expressed remorse and regret. 'We hope this judgment brings the closure to the case,' he said.

Distraught AVUT activists sought another review. They felt that the top court's judgment showed an 'unwarranted leniency' towards the men, whose conviction had been 'upheld by all courts, including this court [the Supreme Court]'.

On 7 November 2016, the real-estate barons too moved the Supreme Court, seeking to unseal the Rs 160 crore Uphaar Cinema property. Appearing for Sushil Ansal, senior lawyer Ram Jethmalani, in his inimitable style argued that his client was not the 'occupier' of Uphaar Cinema nor did he owe any duty of care towards those who came to watch the movie on the fateful day so as to give rise to any civil or criminal liability for the breach of any such duty. Another senior lawyer Sushil Kumar, appearing for Gopal Ansal, adopted a similar line of argument. He too contended that his client had nothing to do with the cinema or the management of its affairs, as on the date of the unfortunate fire incident. They relied on the fact that the cinema was owned by GPTA Pvt. Ltd and later by Ansal Theatres & Clubotels Pvt. Ltd, which alone could be said to be the occupiers of the cinema at the relevant point of time.

Sushil Ansal was its managing director only till 21 November 1983. He had retired from the board of directors on 17 October 1988. Even Gopal, who took over as managing director after his elder brother stepped down, had retired from the board on 17 October 1988, whereafter he exercised no control over the cinema or its management. Their lawyers argued that this didn't earn them what in retrospect is the dubious distinction of being the 'occupier[s] of the cinema'.

Gopal Ansal had no doubt resumed the directorship of the company for a period of six months in December 1994, but was concerned only with the business of the clubs being run by the company. This implied that neither Sushil nor Gopal was the occupier of the cinema on the date of the incident, which meant that no civil or criminal liability could be raised against them, the lawyers reiterated. Rejecting the move to unseal the property, the Supreme Court had stated in its order:

> What is important is whether the premises in question was sufficiently and not exclusively under the control of accused, and for being in such control, ownership of the premises is not a condition precedent. An occupier may be in control of the premises even when he does not own the same whether fully or jointly with others. It is also not necessary that the control must be full and all pervasive. It follows that if there are more than one occupiers of a building, and each one neglects the duty to care, the liability whether civil or criminal will fall on all of them.

While the issue was being heard in the apex court, the Delhi High Court in May 2017 upheld the trial court's order to frame the charge of 'tampering with evidence' against the brothers. Justice Siddharth Mridul held that the brothers were 'in real and effective control of the theatre and management of the company'. Holding them responsible for various structural deviations, the court said they 'connived' with administrative authorities and corrupted them to utilize every corner of the building for more profits, without concern for the safety of the patrons.

'An entrepreneur who corrupts the official of the

government is a menace to the society,' the judge said, sentencing them to two years but underlining that the two-year jail term was 'not sufficient' for incidents like this.

During one of the hearings in October 2012, Sushil Ansal apologized to Neelam Krishnamoorthy. 'He stood up and apologized with folded hands for the loss of my two children,' said Neelam. This was for the first time in fifteen years that the Ansals had apologized for the incident. In the past she had received threats and intimidation for pursuing the case.

As of September 2017, the fine money has been paid and is lying with the court's registry. Gopal surrendered on 20 March 2017 to serve the remainder of his sentence in jail.

The case has had a roller-coaster ride during the past two decades. While all the three courts had confirmed that the Ansals were guilty of negligence and were 'only interested in making money', one brother was allowed to walk free with a fine and the younger one went on to complete another six months of his sentence.

Both of them escaped the stringent charge of culpable homicide not amounting to murder which could have fetched them life terms. The Ansal brothers, who have been called a 'menace', also managed to avoid the two-year jail term prescribed as the maximum punishment for the offence of causing death due to negligence.

On the other hand, the victims and their dear ones seem to have been failed by the system. After twenty years of relentlessly fighting for justice, Neelam now feels dejected as the system proved once again that rich people can get away with anything by paying money, while ordinary citizens bear the suffering all their lives. She feels that the 'accused-friendly system' has failed her and many others like her. 'I am very much disappointed. Twenty years back, I lost faith in God and 20 years later in judiciary . . . I have spent more years fighting this case than I got to spend with my children. But I couldn't get peace for my children. I will never have peace,' says Neelam, who spearheaded the campaign to get justice for the victims of the tragedy. Her husband too has echoed her sentiments. Neelam has articulated her disappointment in no uncertain terms:

> I regret having pursued the Uphaar cinema fire tragedy case so vigorously in the courts for 18 years. I should have just gone out and killed those responsible for the death of my two children and 57 others. I would have pleaded insanity, exactly what Jethmalani accuses me of. By now, I would have finished serving my sentence as well. But I chose law. And this law has let me down.[2]

Senior advocate Tulsi had advised the couple to get organized if they wanted to take on the builder lobby. Nine of the twenty-eight affected families got together to form the AVUT. 'We got in touch with other people after reading obituaries in the newspapers. People who met us on our long fight too put us in touch with others who had suffered,' said Neelam, who has lost count of the number of applications she has filed during her eighteen-year-long battle for justice. The other affected families too feel that justice eludes them. They are disillusioned with Gopal Ansal getting a mere year in prison and his brother Sushil being reprieved, given his old age and medical condition. 'We got convictions from all three courts and yet there is no sentence to them. We didn't want compensation, but punishment for the culprits,' said Naveen Sawhney, who has always made it a point to attend each and every hearing—around 5000 in total—over eighteen years of proceedings. Sawhney had lost his twenty-one-year-old daughter Tarika in the Uphaar fire tragedy.

Experts too felt that the Supreme Court had failed to send out a strong message of deterrence to companies involved in cases of corporate negligence. Three of the top criminal law experts in the country—former additional solicitor general of India Siddharth Luthra and noted senior advocates Majeed Memon and Aman Lekhi—felt that in such cases of corporate negligence, the accused owed a non-delegable duty of care to their customers and both the brothers should have been tried for culpable homicide instead of negligence under Section 304(A) of the IPC.[3] As per Lekhi:

In the Uphaar case, it is not like victims had any urgent need of money as such, the question here was to actually set the example and hold those who were responsible for this contingency to book and ensure similar contingencies do not happen in future . . . as far as age is concerned, consistency is absolutely basic to judicial pronouncements. The age is not something which is that high for the court to be indulgent.

Corporate negligence has probably caused most of the 'man-made' disasters that have occurred in India—be it the Bhopal gas disaster, the Uphaar tragedy or the AMRI Hospital fire incident.

Despite the history of accidents, lax fire-safety measures, a weak regulatory regime and ineffective laws, the country has not learnt anything. Little has changed about India's corporate landscape.

The judicial system of the country failed to provide a strong deterrent to check such crimes. The mild punishments meted out to offenders did little to deter other companies from flouting safety norms. Cases that took decades to resolve did not persuade potential lawbreakers to mend their ways. Companies still manage to take advantage of the system and tweak rules. After any such incident, furious debates take place for months together, innumerable articles and reports are published, and social activism is at its best, but ultimately the struggle for change is reflected on paper only.

The country's lax laws—which punish negligence resulting in death with outdated penalties and just two years of imprisonment, as seen in the Uphaar case—need amendment. Improved safety standards and an effective regulatory regime are the need of the hour. The enforcement of laws is as important as their enactment, especially when such laws deal with the safety and security of citizens and create continuing obligations that call for constant vigil by the administration. Perhaps in this regard, the Uphaar case will be an eye-opener.

Criminal lawyer and member of Parliament K.T.S. Tulsi, who represented the families of the Uphaar victims, hoped 'the verdict will create requisite respect for observance of safety measures by cinema halls and ensure government officials are more careful in their monitoring'.

Expressing solidarity with the victims, Delhi's ruling Aam Aadmi Party had 'raised extremely serious questions [about] the way criminal justice is delivered' in the country. 'The final outcome in the case, which lingered on for 18 years, has led to the public impression that it is a travesty of justice, given the scale of tragedy and magnitude of negligence which was a result of political-bureaucratic-corporate nexus,' the Arvind Kejriwal government had said in a series of tweets.[4]

More than two decades have passed, yet the spectre of Uphaar still haunts the people who were associated with it. The eighteen-year-old tea vendor who had carried mattresses in a bid to rescue the victims is popularly known as Guptaji today. He fought his own court battle for a decade to keep his stall open. 'For two years after the fire, the municipal corporation shut down my shop. I could not send my son to school because of the court costs,' he said. Guptaji's shop and a small room next to the basement remain the only parts of Uphaar that are opened every day amidst the rows of closed offices and shops. 'I still pay the Ansals rent for my shop,' he said.

Over the years, Guptaji has watched all the memorial functions in the park outside the cinema: 'Every time I see the families, I remember the cries of the screaming child thrown down by his parents.'

7

Defending Freedom of Speech

The Right to Offend

'If the freedom of speech is taken away then dumb and silent we may be led, like sheep to the slaughter.'

—George Washington

The news of Shiv Sena supremo Bal Thackeray's death brought Mumbai, the economic capital of India, to a virtual standstill, with businesses shutting down completely and taxis going off the roads. While Thackeray's supporters mourned his death on 17 November 2012, many others were disturbed by the bandh. Some took to various social networking sites to express their anger. Twenty-one-year-old Shaheen Dhadha was one of them. She expressed what she felt, without any malice. In her Facebook post, she wrote:

With all respect, every day, thousands of people die, but still the world moves on. Just due to one politician died a natural death, everyone just goes bonkers. They should know, we are

135

resilient by force, not by choice. When was the last time, did anyone showed some respect or even a two-minute silence for Shaheed Bhagat Singh, Azad, Sukhdev or any of the people because of whom we are free-living Indians? Respect is earned, given, and definitely not forced. Today, Mumbai shuts down due to fear, not due to respect.

Shaheen's friend Renu Srinivasan liked her post and commented: 'Everyone know it's done because of fear!!! We agree that he has done a lot of good things. also we respect him, it doesn't make sense to shut down everything! Respect can be shown in many other ways!' Both of them hardly knew that being vocal in a democratic country would land them in jail. Soon state machinery swung into action and the Palghar Police took both the girls into custody and charged them under various provisions of the Information Technology (IT) Act, 2002. The two young women had a bitter time.

'I have never been to a police station before. I looked around and there were people staring at me. The place was so intimidating. And I was put through all this only because I chose to express my opinion,' said Renu.[1]

Far away, another twenty-one-year-old Shreya Singhal was quite perturbed with this development . . . She was shocked when she found out about the arrest. Memories welled up.

In 2011–12, award-winning political cartoonist and anti-corruption and Internet freedom crusader Aseem Trivedi was arrested on charges of sedition, cybercrime, and insulting the national flag, the Indian Parliament and the Constitution through his work. Trivedi's 'Cartoons against Corruption' website, which featured caricatures mocking the Parliament and corruption in high places, was banned by the Mumbai Police. Amit Katarnayea, a legal adviser working for a Mumbai-based NGO, had approached the police in December 2011 with his complaint against Trivedi's allegedly derogatory sketches, depicting the national emblem and the Parliament in a bad light. The complainant said that the offending cartoons were uploaded on social networking sites too, thereby hurting the sentiments of the nation. Trivedi was produced before the court. The court asked him if he had sought any counsel to represent him. His reply was as follows:

I do not need any counsel. I do not even remember on which sketches of mine the police have arrested me. The police have arrested me for expressing my anger against the government. And if I am an accused by expressing my views, then yes in that case I prefer to be behind bars than to enjoy my freedom in this way.[2]

In 2012, forty-five-year-old Ravi, a small-scale industrialist in Puducherry, was arrested for posting 'offensive' messages on the microblogging site Twitter, targeting the Union finance minister P. Chidambaram's son Karti Chidambaram. Ravi was arrested under Section 66(A) of the IT Act. He had allegedly posted messages on Twitter stating that Karti Chidambaram had amassed more wealth than Robert Vadra, the son-in-law of Congress president Sonia Gandhi.

There were many such instances. Shreya Singhal was convinced that a particular provision in the law was being misused. Section 66(A) of the IT Act gave police the powers to arrest anyone for sending offensive messages from a mobiles phone, tablet or computer; the punishment for such an offence could go up to three years in jail. What message was construed as 'offensive' or 'menacing' or meant for the purpose of causing annoyance, inconvenience, etc. was left to the subjective discretion of policemen.

Over the years, the police had invoked this provision to arrest several people, including a cartoonist, a professor, students and industrialists, particularly when they posted content against politicians.

In April 2012, the West Bengal government used Section 66(A) against a professor of Jadavpur University for circulating emails that mocked Chief Minister Mamata Banerjee. Ambikesh Mahapatra and his neighbour were arrested for circulating a cartoon lampooning Banerjee which was based on a scene from Satyajit Ray's popular children's detective movie *Sonar Kella*.[3]

A month later, the Mumbai Police arrested two Air India cabin crew members, Mayank Mohan Sharma and K.V.J. Rao, for allegedly posting indecent jokes about politicians and for insulting the national flag. While they claimed to have merely circulated what was already present online, both spent twelve days in jail and were suspended from work till the charges were dropped.[4] Kishori Sharma, Bansi Lal and Moti Lal Sharma were arrested and sent to jail for forty days because they had been tagged in a blasphemous video on Facebook and one of them had commented on it.[5]

In August 2013, writer Kanwal Bharti was arrested for posting a message on Facebook criticizing the Uttar Pradesh government for suspending an IAS officer Durga Shakti

Nagpal.[6] Rajeesh Kumar, a CPI (M) worker, was arrested for posting 'abusive' comments and photos on Facebook about Prime Minister Narendra Modi.

In 2014, Devu Chodankar was arrested for posting a comment saying that the then prime minister–elect Narendra Modi will start a holocaust in India. He had posted this comment on a forum on Facebook.[7] A Class XI student from Bareilly was arrested by the Rampur Police for sharing an 'objectionable' post on Facebook against senior Samajwadi Party leader and state urban development minister Azam Khan. A team of crime-branch sleuths picked him up from his house and he was kept in judicial custody for fourteen days.

'It dawned on me that someone had to do something to stop this gross injustice and perverse use of laws . . . If this goes on, we will become a mute society,' Shreya Singhal said.[8]

Most Indians who have access to the Internet widely voice their opinions and concerns through social media. The same thoughts and opinions, if voiced on other media (newspapers, television, etc.), would not have been prosecuted, which is what the grossly misused Section 66(A) was being used for. The Internet is a popular medium for people to express themselves and such expression is our right, one that must be cherished and protected.

'If you say something in a newspaper or on TV, that's fine, but if you say it on Facebook, you get arrested . . . I think there are so many people in India who are tech-savvy and very vocal about their views. It's a natural revolution,' felt the young lady, who became the first person to challenge Section 66(A) of the IT Act, 2002, in the Supreme Court.

She had a heated discussion on the issue with her mother Manali Singhal, a Supreme Court lawyer, who had then advised her to file a PIL.

The Letter of the Law

There have been many cases where Section 66(A) was misused and the subsequent arrests drew much outcry. In most of the cases slapped against persons for posting offensive views on social networking sites, the police had invariably invoked provisions under two different laws—Sections 153 and 505 of the IPC along with Section 66(A) of the IT Act. While offences under the cyber law were bailable, it was under the criminal law that the police arrested the persons for offensive posts. Section 153(A) provides for registration of a case against a person who gives a statement either in writing or orally that incites communal riots or provokes communal tension or enmity between communities. It is punishable with imprisonment from six months to one year with fine. Section 505 punishes persons who spread rumours through their statements in order to cause public disorder with imprisonment up to three years.

Section 66(A) was not part of the original IT Act enacted during the National Democratic Alliance (NDA) government in 2000. The United Progressive Alliance (UPA) government had amended the Act in 2009 and brought Section 66(A) into force on 27 October 2009. At that time Veerappa Moily was the law minister and A. Raja was the minister for information technology.[9]

Freedom of Speech

After spending three years studying astrophysics at the University of Bristol in the UK, Shreya Singhal had returned to India to study law. Her return coincided with several high-profile arrests of people who had exercised their right to freedom of speech online.

Perturbed by the arrest of two young women in Palghar, Shreya, with the help of two lawyers, Ninad Laud and Ranjeeta Rohatgi, filed a PIL in the Supreme Court in 2012. The petition urged the court to declare Section 66(A) of the IT Act unconstitutional on the grounds that it primarily violated the fundamental right of free speech and expression guaranteed by the Constitution of India.[10]

The then chief justice Altamas Kabir had wondered why nobody had so far challenged the particular provision of the IT Act. He asked Singhal, the granddaughter of the late judge Sunanda Bhandare, to send a copy of the petition to the late attorney general G.E. Vahanvati and also involve the Maharashtra government in the matter. The late chief justice of India had voiced concern over people being arrested for posting allegedly offensive messages on websites.

Challenging the constitutionality of the much-abused provision, the petition stated that the 'very basis of Section 66A—that it has given rise to new forms of crimes—is incorrect, and that Sections 66B to 67C and various Sections of the Indian Penal Code were good enough to deal with all these crimes'.

Another petition was filed by industry lobby Internet and Mobile Association of India (IAMAI) against the arbitrary powers that the IT Act conferred on the government to remove user-generated content.

A clutch of petitions, including one by Singhal, said that Section 66(A) infringed the fundamental right to free speech and expression and is not saved by any of the eight subjects covered in Article 19(2) of the Constitution. According to the lawyers, the causing of annoyance, inconvenience, danger, obstruction, insult, injury, criminal intimidation, enmity, hatred or ill will are all outside the purview of Article 19(2). They said that the provision was vague as no attempt had been made by the legislators to define the offences under Section 66(A), which had resulted in the arrests of innocent people.

Section 66(A) was not well defined, and phrases such as 'grossly offensive' and 'menacing character' were subjective. While verbally abusing a person who is physically present in front of the abuser was not a crime, if someone abused a person over the phone or an electronic device, it was a crime as per Section 66(A). It was a logically inconsistent section. A vague law can be abused by the police and can be used as per their whims and fancies.

People who allegedly violated this provision of the law were not told clearly on which side of the line they fall; it allowed the authorities to be as arbitrary and whimsical as they liked. The enforcement of the legal provision would really be an insidious form of censorship which impaired a core value contained in Article 19(1)(a) of the Constitution, the petition said. In addition, the section had a chilling effect on the freedom of speech and expression, Shreya Singhal argued.

Article 19(1)(a) gives people the right to speech and

expression whereas Article 19(2) accords the state the power to impose 'reasonable restrictions' on the exercise of this right for reasons such as interest of the sovereignty and integrity of the country, security of the state, friendly relations with foreign states, public order, decency or morality, defamation or incitement to an offence.

The provision was titled 'punishment for sending offensive messages through communication service' and included information shared via a 'computer resource or a communication device' known to be 'false, but for the purpose of causing annoyance, inconvenience, danger, obstruction, insult, injury, criminal intimidation, enmity, hatred or ill will'.

Pankaj Bafna, a lawyer who deals with cybercrime, said, 'How will one know what will be offensive for another person?' Lawyer Mahesh Jethmalani said, 'An objective criterion must be laid down about what is offensive.'

Senior lawyer Soli Sorabjee, appearing for Singhal, argued that 'unless there is a judicial sanction as a prerequisite to the setting into motion the criminal law with respect to freedom of speech and expression, the law as it stands is highly susceptible to abuse and for muzzling free speech in the country'.

The petitioners also contended that their rights under Articles 14 and 21 of the Constitution were breached inasmuch as there is no intelligible differentia between those who use the Internet and those who by words spoken or written use other mediums of communication. The gist of the plea was to punish somebody because he uses a particular medium of communication is itself a discriminatory object and would fall foul of Article 14 in any case.

However, Additional Solicitor General Tushar Mehta defended the provision, arguing that the legislature is in the best position to understand and appreciate the needs of the people and the mere possibility of abuse did not render the entire provision unconstitutional. Stating that the penal provisions of the IT Act were not intended to curb freedom of speech, he said that instead, Section 66(A) was designed to fight cybercrime.

The court will, therefore, interfere with the legislative process only when a statute is clearly violative of the rights conferred on the citizen under Part-III of the Constitution, he contended.

Putting forth his argument, Mehta lamented that there is a presumption in favour of the enactment. Further, the court would so construe a statute to make it workable and in doing so can read into it or read down the provisions that are impugned. To buttress his submissions, he said:

> [The] mere possibility of abuse of a provision cannot be a ground to declare a provision invalid . . . Loose language may have been used in Section 66A to deal with novel methods of disturbing other people's rights by using the internet as a tool to do so. Further, vagueness is not a ground to declare a statute unconstitutional if the statute is otherwise legislatively competent and non-arbitrary.

The Judgment

In a landmark judgment expanding the contours of free speech to the Internet, the Supreme Court on 24 March

2015 struck down the draconian Section 66(A) of the IT Act, which authorized the police to arrest anyone for social media posts which were construed 'offensive' or 'menacing'. A bench comprising justices J. Chelameswar and R.F. Nariman declared the sweeping law as unconstitutional as it violated the freedom of speech and expression guaranteed under Article 19(1)(a) of the Constitution and was not saved by Article 19(2), which imposes 'reasonable restrictions' on the exercise of the right.

The top court termed Section 66(A) 'open ended, undefined, and unconstitutionally vague', with the words used in the text of the provision being 'nebulous in meaning'. The court said that nothing short of quashing the law 'in its entirety' would suffice since Section 66(A) 'arbitrarily, excessively and disproportionately' invaded the right to free speech, right to dissent and right to know, and had a 'chilling effect' on constitutional mandates.

According to the Supreme Court, 'it is not open to the state to curtail freedom of speech to promote the general public interest'. Justice Nariman, writing for the bench, said that this law had 'no proximate relationship to public order' and failed to pass muster on the 'clear and present danger' test.

'Clear and present danger' constitutes a doctrine adopted by the Supreme Court of the United States to determine under what circumstances limits can be placed on First Amendment freedoms of speech, press or assembly. The issue found its way to the US Supreme Court in the case of *Schenck v. United States*, 249 US 47 (1919). It was the court's first important decision in the area of free speech. Justice Oliver Wendell Holmes wrote the opinion of the unanimous court, which sided with the government. He, in this case, enunciated the clear and present danger test as the following:

> The most stringent protection of free speech would not protect a man in falsely shouting fire in a theatre and causing a panic. It does not even protect a man from an injunction against uttering words that may have all the effect of force. *Gompers v. Buck's Stove & Range Co.*, 221 U. S. 418, 439. The question in every case is whether the words used are used in such circumstances and are of such a nature as to create a clear and present danger that they will bring about the substantive evils that Congress has a right to prevent. It is a question of proximity and degree.

Although the US Constitution's First Amendment protects freedom of speech, any speech that poses a 'clear and present danger' to the public or government loses this protection. The classic example is that shouting 'Fire!' in a crowded theatre is not protected speech.

Quoting from the Preamble to the Indian Constitution, the Supreme Court judgment in the case filed by Shreya Singhal emphasized the 'paramount significance' of the 'cardinal value' of the liberty of thought, expression and belief. In its 123-page judgment, the court also upheld the right to dissent on the Internet. It underlined that Section 66(A) was cast so widely that virtually any opinion on any subject would be covered by it, as any 'serious opinion dissenting with the mores of the day would be caught within its net'.

An assurance by the NDA government to the court that Section 66(A)—brought into the statute by the UPA-II in

2009—will be administered in a reasonable manner failed to impress the bench. The bench said that governments may come and go but Section 66(A) will go on forever and that what is otherwise invalid cannot be saved by assurances.

'An assurance from the present government even if carried out faithfully would not bind any successor government. It must, therefore, be held that Section 66A must be judged on its own merits without any reference to how well it may be administered,' the bench said, ruling that it was unconstitutional and failed to qualify under the umbrella of 'reasonable restriction'. It maintained that the section 'made no distinction between a mere discussion or advocacy of a particular point of view, which may be annoying or inconvenient or grossly offensive to some, and incitement by which such words lead to an imminent causal connection with public disorder, security of state, etc.'. The bench further noted that 'what may cause annoyance or inconvenience to one may not cause annoyance or inconvenience to another'.

The judges, however, upheld the government's power to create separate offences for the cyber world and declared as constitutional Sections 69(A) and 79(3)(b), under which blocking orders and take-down notices are issued by the government to websites to remove certain objectionable content in accordance with guidelines. The court said the guidelines provided necessary safeguards.

While it is Section 66(A) that has garnered maximum attention, the judgment also considered the validity of other provisions of the IT Act like Sections 69(A) and 79, along with the rules made thereunder. Section 69(A) and the Information Technology (Procedure and Safeguards for

Blocking for Access of Information by Public) Rules, 2009, authorize the Central government to block or order an intermediary (such as Facebook, YouTube or any Internet or telecom service provider) to block public access to any content generated, transmitted, stored, etc. in any computer resource, if it is satisfied that such content is likely to create communal disturbance, social disorder or affect friendly relations with foreign states and India's defence and sovereignty, etc.

However, the court said that the intermediaries will not be liable if they fail to take down content upon request from third parties. 'This is for the reason that otherwise it would be very difficult for intermediaries like Google, Facebook, etc. to act when millions of requests are made and the intermediary is then to judge as to which of such requests are legitimate and which are not,' the court said in its judgment.

With regard to Section 69(A), the court held that it is a narrowly drawn provision with several safeguards, noting that content could be blocked only when the Central government is satisfied that it is necessary to do so and that the provision facilitates a hearing before a committee to determine the necessity of blocking the content.

Recalling his experiences while working on the case, lawyer Ninad Laud said, 'The one that remains etched in my memory is the comment by Chief Justice Kabir when I mentioned the writ petition for urgent listing. He said, "I was waiting for someone to come with this", before proceeding to list the matter at 2 p.m. on the same day.'

The single biggest impact of the case is that there is now fluency in the jurisprudence of free speech with much-needed clarity. One can challenge the contaminated aspects of censorship. The judgment validates the right to disagree and oppose and even annoy, all without the fear of the state meddling in.

Apart from striking down an outrageously vague and badly drafted provision, the judgment surely did clear the air on the availability of the freedom of speech and expression on online media. But it is this dictum by Justice Nariman that will hold the citizens of this country in good stead for times to come:

> There are three concepts which are fundamental in understanding the reach of this most basic of human rights. The first is discussion, the second is advocacy, and the third is incitement. Mere discussion or even advocacy of a particular cause howsoever unpopular is at the heart of Article 19(1)(a). It is only when such discussion or advocacy reaches the level of incitement that Article 19(2) kicks in.

In a way, the verdict rejects the censorship law passed by the supreme body, the Parliament, as unconstitutional. It underlines the idea that the state has a very limited space to restrain the right to free speech, emphasizing that it can restrain the same only in extraordinarily exceptional circumstances. The judgment was praised by people from all walks of life—from the common man to the best legal brains in the country.

The apex court defended the Constitution's ideals of tolerance with a sense of vivacity and integrity, and provided clarity. Now one can challenge the censorship that pervades the Indian state. It affords citizens the right to freely express themselves, to dissent and to oppose, and to offend and to annoy, free from substantial interference from the state.

Shreya Singhal, whose name will be recorded in history for her spirited fight, considers the judgment a triumph for free speech, and has said the following:

> Section 66A was a draconian law, and conferred wide, unfettered power to arrest citizens. It acted as a gag on the fundamental right to free speech and expression. Striking it down was a great victory for India as a democracy. The judgment has had a great impact on the way people use the Internet. The users are protected and hence feel more comfortable to express themselves over the Internet, and thus help democracy evolve.

Laud, who drafted the petition for Singhal, felt that the judgment, by allowing people to fearlessly express unpopular views, as long as they do not lead to the incitement of public disorder, was a step in the right direction. He further said:

> However, the ruling that restrictions on freedom of speech can vary from medium to medium, such as online and print media, is an 'intelligible differentia' between the two mediums of communication for which separate offences can certainly be created by legislation, as suggested by Justice Nariman. Hence Parliament can surely make a distinct law on online speech but it would do well not to make it vague and not one that penalizes expression of

merely unpopular views, lest it meet the same fate as that of Section 66A.

The ruling was widely welcomed by free-speech campaigners. The National Association of Software and Service Companies (NASSCOM), the IT lobby group which was a direct stakeholder in this case, said that the 'Internet as a medium is meant to be free and transcend territorial borders with minimal regulation and monitoring.'

Faisal Farooqui, CEO of MouthShut.com, whose petition was also heard along with Singhal's, said that this verdict will lead to the transformation of the Indian economy into a digital economy. '[The] Internet is not just about things like e-commerce, it is also about expression,' he said, adding that 'nobody would like to host libellous content, but the scrapped law wanted us to decide on libel and defamation, which is a very vague and subjective term'.[11]

The then law minister Veerappa Moily, who had refused to be drawn into the controversy over Section 66(A), was diplomatic. He said that the law should be dynamic and evolve with time to meet the exigencies peculiar to a particular time.

Kapil Sibal, who succeeded Moily as the country's law minister, also welcomed the judgment. However, he said that 'Section 66A is not the culprit as it is a bailable offence. The police used to invoke provisions of IPC to effect the arrests. So, one should be well advised to still exercise restraint while exercising free speech on social networking sites.'[12]

According to Sibal, in an ideal world free speech would not attract the provisions of the IPC, even if it involved the severest criticism of political leaders. He then underscored that if the free speech in question has an intention to cause public disorder or communal disharmony, impacting national integrity and friendly relations with other countries, then the IPC provisions should come into the picture. He further added:

> The challenge before the country now is the discretion provided to the police in registering a case under IPC provisions branding a statement offensive under Sections 153 and 505 of IPC. The distinction between a pure free speech from offensive statements by the police is the challenge. And it is this discretion with police that is often misused.[13]

The public outrage over state interference in free speech, however, hasn't ended as the police has gone on to arrest more than 3000 people illegally even after it was struck down by the Supreme Court in March 2015. According to the National Crime Records Bureau (NCRB), 3137 people were arrested under the section in 2015 against 2423 the previous year. The number has only gone up. That is the irony.[14]

Having said this, how do we guard free speech against abuse and misuse in a multiracial, multicultural country such as ours? Critics feel that every law in our country is vulnerable to exploitation. The mere prospect of abuse should not have been the grounds for removing an essential provision in totality.

Let's admit that free speech is susceptible to abuse, and would lead to communal disharmony, political vendetta or religious intolerance. We are not yet prepared for such an absolute and unrestrained right. What we need to ponder over is how we can exercise this right to free speech without hurting anyone.

Hence, there is a need for the Parliament to come up with an alternative to Section 66(A) to ensure that a person enjoys his fundamental right to speech and, at the same time, understands the responsibilities attached to it. In today's times, when riots are caused due to hateful content going viral on social media, we do need checks and balances to ensure that this right is not misused.

That said, this truly landmark judgment represents a rare instance of the court adopting the extreme step of declaring a censorship law passed by the Parliament as altogether illegitimate. It has clarified the scope of the right available to us to express ourselves freely and has given the state limited authority to restrain this freedom in only the most exceptional of circumstances. As Justice Nariman's decision has highlighted, the liberty of thought and expression is not merely an aspirational ideal. It is also 'a cardinal value that is of paramount significance under our constitutional scheme'.[15]

8

Lily Thomas v. Union of India

The Coup to Save Democracy

'Democracy is a faith in the spiritual possibilities of not a privileged few but of every human being.'

—Sarvepalli Radhakrishnan

When Lily Thomas took up the fight for a clean political system in the country, she was already seventy-eight. Age was just a number for her.

Many shared her sentiments, but it was her courage, grit and conviction that drove her to take the initiative to stop criminals from entering politics. It is not that she wanted to prove a point. She was neither driven by monetary gains nor power nor fame. It was a call for 'clean politics and clean politicians'. In her quest to keep convicts out of politics, she had to fight a long-drawn legal battle with the government.

It was on her eighty-fifth birthday that she got the best gift—she won the most important case of her life. Big political giants were cut to size when in a landmark judgment in July 2013, the Supreme Court struck down Section 8(4) of the Representation of the People Act (RPA), 1951, as unconstitutional. This meant that a member of Parliament (MP) or a member of the Legislative Assembly (MLA) stood disqualified from public office immediately if convicted by a court for crimes with a punishment of two years or more.

Hailing from Kottayam, Thomas belongs to the first generation of women lawyers in India. She is the first woman to complete LLM from Madras University. After obtaining a law degree, she started her practice in the Madras High Court. In 1960, she moved to Delhi to do her PhD. She started with her research, but dropped out after a few months. 'I realized I was not made for the rigour of academics. So I started practising in the Supreme Court and joined my brother John Thomas who was already practising then,' she recollected.

As a devout and dedicated lawyer, Thomas has been filing petitions since 1964 on different issues. She staunchly believes that it is the responsibility of lawyers to fight through courts to improve the existing laws.

'There is a fundamental flaw in our democracy that inadvertently devalues the judiciary. The Representation of People Act, 1951, encouraged tainted leaders to contest elections. This should never have been permitted,' she said, explaining her reasons for filing the petition.

It all started in 2005 when Thomas, a Supreme Court lawyer working on constitutional law, women's rights and issues of personal liberty, along with advocate Satya Narain Shukla, filed the petition. Thomas was enraged at the idea of convicts getting a stay on their conviction from higher courts, contesting elections and winning them. In her own words:

The primary aim that I had in mind was to ensure that Parliament should be free of criminals and corruption. It is the duty of the Bar to ensure that there is no place for convicts. With my training and education as an advocate, I would consider it a serious dereliction of duty if I did not take up these issues.[1]

She added that allowing criminals to contest as politicians is an insult to the parliamentary system.

The petition was rejected by Chief Justice R.C. Lahoti twice on the grounds that it was not substantial and foolproof. Disillusioned but undeterred, Thomas worked hard and it was only on her third attempt that Justice Lahoti admitted the Public Interest Litigation (PIL).

After consent had been obtained from the office of the late attorney general G.E. Vahanvati, the matter was assigned to the bench comprising justices A.K. Patnaik and S.J. Mukhopadhaya.

The stakes were high. A lack of accountability, the rising trend of scams and frauds, corruption, an increasing incidence of criminals in politics and the misuse of power by politicians had gradually become the order of the day, most of it made possible by the manoeuvring of legal loopholes by politicians to retain political hold. The wrongdoers were getting away with it all. It was becoming a formidable threat to our constitutional integrity.

Section 8(4) of the RPA was the central point of the legal tussle. The provision gave protection to convicted lawmakers against disqualification from Parliament and state legislative assemblies on the ground of pendency of appeal against their conviction in the higher courts. This broadly meant that the provision allowed a convict to file an appeal in a higher court and get his conviction stayed for the purpose of contesting elections. It was this loophole in the law that Thomas wanted to fix and replace with something that would bring about a desired change.

She took it upon herself to reform politics. The underpinning of Thomas's petition was that there should be no place for convicts in the Parliament, as it was a temple of democracy and public service. Soon Lucknow-based NGO Lok Prahari joined her, which strengthened her resolve to clean up the electoral system and also uphold the integrity of the Parliament. The two PILs issued called for the Supreme Court to declare Section 8(4) of the RPA illegal and ultra vires the Constitution. Both petitions were clubbed together by the court.

Constitutional expert and senior Supreme Court lawyer Fali Nariman played an instrumental role in the case. He argued the matter for both the petitioners. It took almost eight years for the apex court to decide the matter, which was considered to be of utmost importance. 'I asked Nariman because I didn't have the requisite knowledge to do the same. His experience, stature and depth in such matters were required. I told him that he has got a responsibility to fight the case. He accepted,' Thomas recalls.

Once the veteran lawyer agreed to fight the case, Thomas's team members sat with his office staff to jointly work on the case, recalls Nischal Kumar Neeraj, Supreme Court advocate-on-record and one of the team members.

The facts that were considered during the hearing

included how the Constituent Assembly, while drafting the Constitution, intended to lay down some disqualifications for MPs and MLAs. Two significant provisions pertaining to disqualification were adopted—Article 102(1) and Article 191(1) of the Constitution.

While Article 102(1) laid down the disqualifications for membership of either house of Parliament, Article 191(1) provided disqualifications for membership of the Legislative Assembly or Legislative Council of the state. Parliament also provided, in Chapter III of the RPA, for the disqualification of membership of Parliament and state legislatures under different charges including corruption, violence against women and sexual offences, customs violation, the illegal use of drugs and inciting communal hatred.

Sections 7 and 8 in Chapter III of the RPA were focus areas in the writ petitions for this case. The term 'disqualified' was defined in Clause(B) of Section 7 of the RPA. Section 8 of the RPA deals with disqualification on conviction for certain offences: A person convicted for any offence and sentenced to imprisonment for varying terms under Sections 8(1), (2) and (3) shall be disqualified from the date of conviction and shall continue to be disqualified for a further period of six years post his or her release. But Section 8(4) of the RPA gives protection to MPs and MLAs as they can continue in office even after conviction if an appeal is filed within three months.

So the legal system for disqualification was always in place, but the provisions of Section 8(4) served as a shield for politicians.

Nariman led the argument for both Thomas and S.N. Shukla,

the general secretary of Lok Prahari. He, among other things, submitted that the opening words of Clause (1) of Articles 102 and 191 of the Constitution make it clear that persons to be elected as MPs or MLAs are on an equal footing as sitting MPs and MLAs so far as disqualifications are concerned. So the sitting members cannot enjoy the special privilege of continuing as members even though they are convicted of the offences.

Nariman further said that when the Constitution provides equality to all, including equality before the law under Article 14, then it is not justified to give protection to the sitting MPs or MLAs and not to aspiring MPs or MLAs. This, according to him, is a clear violation of the right to equality guaranteed by the Constitution.

Additional solicitor generals Siddharth Luthra and Paras Kuhad countered Nariman. They focused on the point that the validity of Section 8(4) has been upheld by the Constitution bench in a previous case.[2] They argued that the purpose of this legal provision was not to give an advantage to sitting MPs and MLAs, but to protect the house. To do so, the Parliament was competent to even enact the provision to temporarily postpone the effect of such disqualification. Luthra's central argument was that if a member was debarred from sitting in the house and participating in the proceedings then two consequences would follow: First, the strength of the membership of the house would be reduced and this would also impact the strength of the political party to which a convicted member may belong. The government in power may survive on a razor-thin majority and the disqualification of even one member may seriously effect its position in the house. Second, a by-election may have to be held, but the exercise might result in complications in case the convicted member gets acquitted by a superior criminal court later.

The reality of the Indian judicial system is that acquittals at the level of appellate courts like the high court are very high. It is for this reason that the Parliament has provided for the deferment of disqualification till the appeal or revision against the conviction is decided by the appellate or the revisional court. Giving a rationale for enacting the saving provision, Paras, who also appeared for the Union of India, supported Luthra's stand.

The Landmark Judgment

It was on 10 July 2013 that the Supreme Court delivered a landmark judgment in the two cases. The judges, A.K. Patnaik and S.J. Mukhopadhaya, struck down as unconstitutional Section 8(4) of the RPA, which allowed convicted lawmakers a three-month period for filing appeal to the higher court and to get a stay on the conviction and sentence.

The judgment warranted immediate and automatic disqualification of charge-sheeted MPs and MLAs from office from the date of conviction for an offence with punishment for two years or more. It also barred those with pending criminal cases from contesting elections. The bench found it unconstitutional that convicted persons could be disqualified from contesting elections but could continue to be MPs and MLAs once elected.

The apex court, however, made it clear that the ruling would not affect serving lawmakers who were facing, or have appealed against, charges because the law could not be enforced retrospectively.

> A reading of the two provisions in Articles 102(1)(e) and 191(1)(e) of the Constitution would make it abundantly clear that Parliament is to make one law for a person to be disqualified for being chosen as, and for being, a Member of either House of Parliament or Legislative Assembly or Legislative Council of the State. Parliament thus does not have the power under Articles 102(1)(e) and 191(1)(e) of the Constitution to make different laws for a person to be disqualified for being chosen as a member and for a person to be disqualified for continuing as a member of Parliament or the State Legislature.

In the judgment, Justice Patnaik said:

> The language of Articles 102(1)(e) and 191(1)(e) of the Constitution is such that the disqualification for both—a person to be chosen as a member of a House of Parliament or the State Legislature and for a person to continue as a member of Parliament or the State Legislature—has to be the same.

The bench held that the provisions of Article 101(3)(a) and 190(3)(a) of the Constitution expressly 'prohibit Parliament to defer the date from which the disqualification will come into effect in case of a sitting member of Parliament or a State Legislature'.

To negate the impact of the decision, the UPA

government led by Prime Minister Manmohan Singh in September the same year brought out an ordinance—the Representation of the People's (Second Amendment and Validation) Bill, 2013. However, Rahul Gandhi, vice president of the Indian National Congress, publicly berated the government's controversial ordinance to shield convicted politicians. In a press meeting, he said that the ordinance is 'complete nonsense. It should be torn up and thrown away.' Subsequently, the government withdrew both the ordinance and the bill within a week.

Now there is a pending PIL in the Supreme Court on why convicts should not be debarred from contesting elections for life.

Impact

It was a watershed judgment that had far-reaching effects. It led to the disqualification of the likes of Lalu Prasad Yadav (Rashtriya Janta Dal or RJD), the then Tamil Nadu chief minister J. Jayalalithaa (All India Anna Dravida Munnetra Kazhagam or AIADMK), Rasheed Masood (Indian National Congress), Jagdish Sharma (Janata Dal-United or JD-U) and many more from contesting elections. Many were found guilty of corruption.[3]

On 1 October 2013, Masood became the first MP to lose his membership of Parliament as he was sentenced to a four-year imprisonment for cheating, forgery and corruption.[4] The conviction in the fodder scam case also resulted in former Bihar chief minister and RJD leader Lalu Prasad's automatic disqualification from Lok Sabha.[5]

Even Jayalalithaa's disqualification as a member of the Legislative Assembly as a result of her conviction in the disproportionate assets case was a fallout of the Lily Thomas judgment. However, her conviction abated after her death on 5 December 2016.

The recent case in this series has been that of the AIADMK general secretary V.K. Sasikala. Earlier in 2017, the Supreme Court set aside Sasikala's acquittal by the Karnataka High Court in the Jayalalithaa disproportionate assets case and restored the trial court conviction of September 2014. This means that even after Sasikala comes out after serving her four-year sentence, she would be disqualified from contesting elections for the next six years in accordance with the Supreme Court's judgment. The trial court had sentenced Sasikala and two others to simple imprisonment for a period of four years each and also imposed a fine of Rs 10 crore each under various provisions of the IPC and the Prevention of Corruption Act.

The Supreme Court played an important role as the custodian of political ethics. Dr Abhishek Singhvi, senior advocate, Congress MP and Congress spokesperson, said the following of the Lily Thomas judgment in my interview with him:

It is significant inasmuch as it judicially corrected what had been long perceived to be an unfair and discriminatorily beneficial classification in favour of sitting legislators which, despite long and sustained criticism from all sections of society, had not received legislative correction. The public sentiment was clearly and unequivocally against this arbitrary carve out in favour of convicted but sitting legislators and the court, as I have long believed it does on diverse issues, rode on that public mood and converted it into a binding judicial corrective.

At its base, the reasoning was strikingly simple and hence alluring. The Constitution prohibited even the standing for election of a convicted legislator. It prescribed conviction as a disqualification. How then could Parliament, merely a law-making delegate of the Constitution, nullify that primordial constitutional mandate, by enacting Section 8(4) of the RPA which stayed the disqualifying effect of conviction for a sitting legislator upon the mere filing of an appeal, without any stay or suspension by a court. On that simple basis, the court declared Section 8(4) unconstitutional. Interestingly, it explicitly refrained from deciding the more obvious point of Article 14 arising on the same facts! The judgment cannot be faulted on equity, common sense, legal principle or societal angst at over-privileged legislators.

'The judiciary very well knows its own limits. The interpretation of law is the function of the judiciary. This judgment will make people think. It will create awareness about constitutional principles,' said Thomas.

The debate over criminals and criminality in politics has been going on for a long time. The reform proposals made by the Election Commission of India have always kept this concern at the forefront. One premise is that the democratic process of the country should not allow criminals to contest elections and hence run the government. The opposing view is that running for elections is every citizen's right and that people should be allowed to decide who they wish to choose.

While the impact of the judgment may be praiseworthy, concerns have been raised about its implications on the stability of governments. Legal experts feel the ruling can be misused to settle personal grudges. Even political parties feel this will encourage the filing of frivolous cases by rivals who want to eliminate candidates from contesting elections. However, others see this as a convenient excuse given by politicians for their own vested interests.

Many feel that the framers of our Constitution envisaged a system of institutional checks and balances. But it is unfortunate that in its attempt to protect the Constitution, the Supreme Court has effectively taken away the Parliament's power to suspend disqualifications on conviction, and arrogated this power to itself.

A mind-numbingly high percentage of Indian politicians have criminal charges pending against them. A survey conducted in June 2013 by the Association of Democratic Reforms and National Election Watch found that as many as 162 MPs out of the 543 Lok Sabha MPs of the 15th Lok Sabha had 522 cases pending against them. Seventy-six out of the 543 MPs were accused of crimes of a very serious nature.

The number of parliamentarians with criminal cases against them has risen in the 16th Lok Sabha, with every third MP-elect facing criminal charges, an analysis of their election affidavits had shown.[6]

An analysis of 541 of the 543 winners in the 2014 Lok Sabha elections showed that 186 or 34 per cent of the newly elected members had disclosed criminal cases against themselves in their affidavits. Of the 186 members, 112 (21 per cent) declared 'serious criminal cases', including those related to murder, attempt to murder, causing communal disharmony, kidnapping, crimes against women, etc.

BJP led the chart in the 2014 elections with as many as ninety-eight winning candidates (35 per cent) out of a total of 282 facing criminal charges. Eight of the forty-four winners (18 per cent) from the Congress, six of the thirty-seven winners (16 per cent) from the AIADMK, fifteen of the eighteen winners (83 per cent) from the Shiv Sena and seven of the thirty-four winners (21 per cent) of the Trinamool Congress also disclosed criminal cases against themselves.

There has been an increasing trend in the number of MPs with a criminal background. In 2004, there were 128 MPs (24 per cent of the total) with pending criminal cases in comparison with 2009, where 162 such MPs (30 per cent) were in the Parliament. [7]

'Crime does not give stability. Ethics give stability. Stability comes from natural justice . . . J.M. Lyngdoh had once referred to corrupt politicians as "cancer of society". Only a clean, "satvic" image of Parliament can provide stability,' Thomas said in an interview to *Frontline* magazine.[8]

She is hopeful that her efforts in the long run will ensure that criminals with political aspirations do not abuse prolonged trials to their advantage. The judgment will likely usher in a new age of democracy and create a new kind of awakening and awareness, especially among the young voters and the future leaders. It's a step towards ensuring an administration and a political system free of corruption.

9

The 1993 Mumbai Blasts

Black Friday

'Though the mills of God grind slowly, yet they grind
  exceeding small;
Though with patience He stands waiting, with exactness
  grinds He all.'

—Henry Wadsworth Longfellow

The Indian judicial system may be known for delays, but there
have been occasions when it has responded even at night. A
case in point is when three judges assembled hurriedly at
3.20 a.m. on 30 July 2015 in courtroom no. 4 of the Supreme
Court to hear lawyers Anand Grover and Yug Chaudhry, who
wanted the judges to set aside the death warrant for Yakub
Abdul Razak Memon. After an unprecedented ninety-minute
hearing that ended a little before dawn at 5 a.m., the bench
comprising justices Dipak Misra, Prafulla Chandra Pant and
Amitava Roy rejected the prayer.

'Stay of death warrant would be a travesty of justice. The plea is dismissed,' held Justice Misra, now the chief justice of India.

The last-ditch fight to stave off the execution was triggered after President Pranab Mukherjee rejected the mercy plea of Yakub, who was the first and only convict sent to the gallows in the 1993 Mumbai blasts case. On 12 March 1993, a series of twelve coordinated explosions had rocked Mumbai, killing 257 and injuring 713 persons.

Three hours later, around 7 a.m. on 30 July 2015, Yakub—the brother of Ibrahim alias Tiger Memon, the chief conspirator of the Mumbai blasts—was hanged in the Nagpur Central Jail. It was the day he turned fifty-three.

Yakub, a chartered accountant by profession, was given the death penalty by a special Terrorist and Disruptive Activities (Prevention) Act (TADA) court in July 2007, which was subsequently confirmed by the Supreme Court for the dozen explosions that ripped through India's financial capital. Yakub was found guilty of criminal conspiracy, arranging money for buying vehicles used by the bombers and organizing air tickets to Dubai for some of them to get trained in arms and ammunition. He was also given life imprisonment for the illegal possession and transportation of arms and ammunition, rigorous imprisonment for fourteen years for possessing explosives with the intent to endanger lives under the TADA Act and rigorous imprisonment for another ten years for aiding, abetting and smuggling arms, ammunitions and explosives into the country under the Explosive Substances Act.

The chain of events that would lead to this gruesome crime

in Mumbai started with an incident in the state of Uttar Pradesh. Tension had been brewing up after the demolition of the Babri Masjid by Hindu kar sevaks on 6 December 1992 in Ayodhya. Widespread communal riots broke out throughout the country, including in Mumbai (then Bombay) which was the worst hit. Both Hindus and Muslims were baying for each other's blood.

In order to take revenge for the demolition, Dubai-based underworld don Dawood Ibrahim Kaskar masterminded the Mumbai attacks with Tiger, one of his most trusted associates. He had sent arms and ammunitions into India for Tiger Memon and his men. Yakub and other co-accused received them through Mumbai's seacoasts. Tiger had also sent some disgruntled Muslim youths to travel to Pakistan via Dubai to receive training so as to spread terror on Indian soil. Both Dawood Ibrahim and Tiger Memon, who are now in safe havens, have been declared 'wanted absconders' in the case.

Black Friday: A Tale of Horror

On 12 March 1993, Mumbai, the busy commercial hub of the country, witnessed unprecedented terrorist attacks which sent shock waves throughout the country. In a span of about two hours, between 1.33 p.m. and 3.40 p.m., a series of twelve bomb explosions took place at twelve different landmark locations. These were the Bombay Stock Exchange, Katha Bazaar, Sena Bhavan, Century Bazaar, Mahim Causeway, Air India Building, Zaveri Bazaar, Sea Rock Hotel, Plaza Cinema, Juhu Centaur Hotel, Sahar Airport (Bay No. 54) and Airport Centaur Hotel.

These serial bombings claimed 257 lives, seriously injured 713 people and destroyed property worth Rs 27 crore. It was the first terror attack on Indian soil in which RDX, an explosive material, was used on a large scale after World War II. Bombs were also planted at other places such as Naigaon Cross Road, Dhanji Street and Sheikh Memon Street, but these were defused in time.

This was the largest coordinated terror attack in India. The objective of the crime was to incite communal violence, weaken the government, disturb social harmony and to break up the social, political and economic order of the country. The conspiracy was originally hatched on or before 6 January 1993 during the first meeting held at the hotel Persian Darbar, Panvel, Mumbai. Thereafter, a series of meetings took place at various different locations including Dubai.

After the FIR was lodged, several arrests were made. The investigations revealed that the original plan was to cripple Mumbai in April during the Shiv Jayanti celebrations, but the same was advanced after one of the accused, Gul Noor Mohammad Sheikh (Gullu), was arrested in March. Gullu was one of the nineteen men handpicked by Tiger and sent across the border for training in arms and bomb-making. He had spilt the beans and confessed to making plans to kill BJP and Shiv Sena corporators.

Around twenty-seven criminal cases were registered at various police stations. The case was cracked by the Mumbai Police within forty-eight hours of the attacks after they found a Maruti van, owned by Rubina Memon, Yakub's sister-in-law, loaded with explosives. This led the police to probe the Memons and subsequently unravel the case.

It took around eight months of investigations for the Mumbai Police to file a single 10,000-page charge sheet against 189 accused, including forty-four absconding accused, on 4 November 1993. Subsequently, the case was transferred to the Central Bureau of Investigation (CBI), which filed nineteen supplementary charge sheets. In the middle of these developments, the TADA court was shifted to a separate building inside the premises of the Arthur Road Central Jail on 1 April 1994. To render speedy justice, in 1995, a special designated TADA court was set up and Special Judge P.D. Kode was nominated to try the Mumbai bomb blast cases.

The first leg of the trial concluded in 2007, during which 687 witnesses were examined. The trial court convicted 100 persons and acquitted twenty-three persons of all the charges. Twenty people were awarded life sentences, while twelve were sentenced to death. One of the notable convictions in the case was that of Bollywood actor Sanjay Dutt.

On 26 July 2007, the TADA court awarded the death sentence to eleven persons, including Yakub, for offences under TADA, the IPC, 1860, the Arms Act, 1959, and the Explosives Act, 1884.

On the day of the judgment, Yakub wore a crisp white shirt and pale blue jeans. He sat in the first row of the benches meant for convicts. As he was held guilty, the otherwise seemingly calm convict shouted at the trial court: 'Oh my lord—forgive this man for he knows not what he does.' Without listening to the rest of the sentence, he rushed out of the courtroom.[1]

'In cases of conspiracy, even if you do not commit the act you will be held liable for conspiracy if evidence proves you are involved in the planning,' the judge had held before awarding the death sentence.

Yakub, the only well-educated member of the Memon family, had consistently maintained that he had returned from hiding because he was innocent. He had once told the trial judge that he had a lot of respect for the Indian authorities before whom he had surrendered in July 1994. His stand was contrary to the CBI's claim that he was arrested on 5 August 1994. 'I feel betrayed. Yet I have not lost faith in truth and justice. I have immense faith in the Constitution,' he had told the designated special trial judge, who recorded his statement under Section 313 of the Code of Criminal Procedure Code (CrPC) on 7 July 2001.

The legal provision allows an accused to personally give an explanation about the circumstances in the evidence against him. Though the recorded statement is not treated as evidence by the court, it can be considered to appreciate the truthfulness or otherwise of the case of the prosecution.

Sanjay Dutt

A part of the consignment of weapons and explosives smuggled into India by Dawood Ibrahim was also delivered to actor Sanjay Dutt, son of yesteryear Bollywood actors, the late Sunil Dutt and Nargis. The consignment included three AK-56 rifles, nine magazines, 450 cartridges, a 9-mm pistol and over twenty hand grenades. The police found that Sanjay had acquired AK-56s from Dawood Ibrahim's younger brother Anees Ibrahim, but had returned two rifles and kept one. Sanjay Dutt had also purchased one 9-mm pistol from a close associate of Dawood Ibrahim. When the news of his involvement came to light, he asked his friend Yusuf Nulwalla to destroy the rifle in his possession. The gun, he claimed, was to protect his family as they had received threats during the Mumbai riots. But he denied having any knowledge of the bomb plot. Sanjay was lucky for not being convicted under TADA. The special court, on 28 November 2006, acquitted him under TADA, but convicted him under the milder Arms Act and handed him a six-year jail sentence. The court said that the actor was not a terrorist and had acquired the gun for self-defence.

On 21 March 2013, the apex court upheld his conviction, but reduced it to five years from the six-year jail term awarded to him in 2006 for the illegal possession of a 9-mm pistol and an AK-56 rifle, which was part of the consignment of weapons and explosives sent to India for the serial blasts. He was also asked to surrender within four weeks to complete his remaining three-and-a-half-year jail term. He had earlier spent eighteen months behind bars.

The Supreme Court Verdict

Around a hundred cross-appeals were filed in the Supreme Court—fifty-one by the accused, including Yakub, against their conviction since 2007 and forty-eight by the State of Maharashtra through the CBI against the acquittals and for the confirmation of the death penalty. After six years, the Supreme Court on 21 March 2013 confirmed the death sentence awarded to Yakub, the main accused, holding him guilty of being the 'driving spirit' in the 1993 Mumbai serial blasts.

A bench of justices P. Sathasivam and B.S. Chauhan also upheld the life sentence awarded to twenty-three others, including police and customs officers; Yakub's brother Essa Memon for conspiracy and allowing his flat at the Al-Hussaini building at Mahim to be used for meetings and storing arms and ammunition; and Rubina Memon for arranging finances and allowing her car to be used by terrorists for carrying arms and explosives.

Writing the judgment, Justice Sathasivam maintained that Pakistan had a major part in the blasts. 'A careful reading of the confessional statements of the convicted accused exposes that a large number of the accused, including the absconders, received training in [the] making of bombs by using RDX and other explosives' in Pakistan.

Noting that Yakub and other members of the Memon family had played a predominant role in the execution of the conspiracy, the judgment stated that the confessions of various co-accused revealed that Tiger Memon had instructed them to stay in touch with Yakub for further instruction.

Yakub had assumed the role of Tiger Memon in India during his absence. As an outcome, Tiger Memon gave the commands to Yakub, who in turn passed them on to the other accused ... Essentially, Yakub Memon's deeds can't be viewed distinct from the act of Tiger Memon, hence both owe an equivalent responsibility for the blasts. They were the architects of the blasts, without whom the plan would never have seen the daylight.

The court observed that there was no direct act attributed to Yakub as far as the parking of the explosive-filled vehicle in different localities was concerned. But it further said that without Yakub being a party too, the explosives and ammunition wouldn't have entered into the country and the executions wouldn't have materialized.

The Memons, including Yakub, were the principle perpetrators of the crime and had fled the country after targeting the underprivileged and easily impressible to accomplish their ulterior motives. Yakub, of course, came back.

Before his arrest, Yakub had come to Kathmandu secretly from Karachi to consult a relative and a lawyer on whether he should return to India and surrender as he and some of his family members were uncomfortable with the Inter-Services Intelligence (ISI). Though he was advised against surrender, he was apprehended before he could board the flight to Karachi by Nepal Police, who sent him to India, according to late B. Raman, former additional secretary in the Cabinet Secretariat. Raman then headed the Pakistan desk in the Research and Analysis Wing (R&AW) when he coordinated the operation to bring back Yakub and other members of the Memon family from Karachi in 1994. Yakub had all through cooperated with the investigating agencies and assisted them by persuading some of his other family members to flee from the protection of the ISI in Karachi to Dubai and surrender to the Indian authorities, Raman had stated.[2]

Yakub fought too many rounds of litigation in the Supreme Court—the appeal, two review petitions, a curative petition and two writ petitions against the warrant of execution of the death sentence. His review petition was dismissed by circulation on 30 July 2013. Soon after, his brother Suleiman filed a mercy petition before President Pranab Mukherjee, which was rejected on 11 April 2014.

Another bench comprising justices J. Khehar and C. Nagappan also dismissed Yakub's second review petition on 9 April 2015 in an open court hearing, as sought by the lone convict. The arguments went on for ten days as against the maximum limit of thirty minutes prescribed by the Supreme Court. Within a month, on 30 April 2015, the Maharashtra government had issued a death warrant, setting 30 July 2015 as the date for Yakub's execution.

Desperate Yakub then moved a curative petition, which was rejected on 21 July 2015. Meanwhile, he sought mercy from Maharashtra Governor C. Vidyasagar Rao and also simultaneously approached the apex court for a stay on his execution till the mercy petition was decided. He claimed that the death warrant was illegal as it had been issued before he had exhausted all his legal avenues of appeal.

While the case dragged on for over two decades, what happened in the last twenty-four hours before his hanging is unprecedented in the annals of the Indian judiciary.

Yakub made another desperate attempt on 28 July by filing another plea challenging the order passed in the curative petition. His lawyers—senior advocates T.R. Andhyarujina and Anand Grover—faulted dismissal of the curative petition by a bench which did not include two of the three judges who had dismissed Yakub's review petition on 9 April.

A day before his scheduled execution on 29 July, Yakub's plea questioning the lack of quorum was taken up by a bench comprising justices Anil R. Dave and Kurien Joseph in courtroom no. 3. It turned out to be an unexpected drama. Stark differences of opinion emerged between the two judges, virtually on every aspect of the matter, and they delivered dissenting orders, necessitating a larger bench.

This prompted Chief Justice H.L. Dattu to set up a larger bench on the same day and he entrusted the task to justices Dipak Misra, Prafulla Chandra Pant and Amitava Roy. They rejected Yakub's prayer for a stay on his death sentence on the grounds that all legal remedies were yet to be exhausted, including the issue of clemency pending before the Maharashtra Governor. The dismissal came around 4.15 p.m. when the bench observed that the President had already rejected his mercy petition on 11 April 2014 and the same was communicated to him on 26 May 2014. The prisoner didn't challenge it, it said, adding that 'how the second mercy petition is going to be dealt with, we are not inclined to go into'. Besides, the apex court held that the curative petition decided by the three senior-most judges cannot be regarded as 'void or inappropriate' and there was nothing wrong in the issuance of the death warrant by the TADA court. Earlier in the day, the Maharashtra Governor had also turned down Yakub's plea seeking a reconsideration of his death sentence.

Dejected Yakub then submitted a second mercy petition, fourteen pages long, to the President, which was rejected late in the evening at around 11 p.m. In yet another last-ditch action, Yakub's lawyers went to meet Chief Justice H.L. Dattu at his residence along with a few others, including activist–lawyer Prashant Bhushan. They were successful in convincing Dattu that Yakub's case deserved to be heard, and so, the final hearing was scheduled in the wee hours, leaving Yakub dangling between hope and despair.

Bhagwandas Road—where the Supreme Court is situated—was bustling with unusual activity on 30 July 2015 at around 3 a.m. in the morning. The case got incessant media coverage throughout the night as well. It was the first time in the history of the Supreme Court that a case was being heard post-midnight inside the court premises.

While the final hearing that would seal Yakub's fate was underway, the then Attorney General Mukul Rohatgi entered the court at 3.15 a.m.; along with him, the judges took their seats at 3.30 a.m. and Grover began his arguments.

He said if the unconfirmed television reports that the President of India had rejected Yakub's petition were true, then no execution could be carried out for a period of fourteen days, a legal requirement held necessary by the Supreme Court to allow the convict to make peace with his god, meet his family, draft his will and settle his affairs. Similar arguments had been made earlier in the day, the only difference being that the request to adhere to the mandatory time period before the execution was made in the context of a mercy petition pending with the Governor. Rohatgi asserted that the proceedings were an abuse of the process of law.

After hearing both the sides patiently for about ninety minutes without any interruption, Justice Misra described the petition before it as an 'exposé of the manipulation of the principle of rule of law'.

Yakub Memon and His Hanging

Yakub was the third of six sons fathered by Abdul Razak Memon. After getting a BCom degree, he went on to become a chartered accountant in 1990. A year later, he set up Mehta & Memon Associates along with a childhood friend, Chetan Mehta. But both parted ways within a year and Yakub set up his independent firm A.R. & Sons in memory of his father. Soon, he diversified into exports and set up another company, Tejrath International, to export meat and meat products to the Gulf and the Middle East.

Yakub also did his MA in English literature and political science in Nagpur Central Jail through the Indira Gandhi National Open University. He passed his second master's degree in political science in December 2014 but the degree was not conferred upon him till his hanging date.[3]

Yakub had stayed awake all night before his hanging. A birthday cake was also sent to him at night. He was taken to the gallows at 6.30 a.m. where he was informed about the verdict. The chief judicial magistrate of Nagpur, M.M. Deshpande, read out the operating part of the TADA court verdict that sentenced Yakub to death before he was hanged at 7 a.m. in Nagpur Central Jail, hardly two hours after a Supreme Court bench rejected his plea to postpone his hanging.

The hangman was a police constable who also executed 26/11 terror convict Mohammed Ajmal Amir Kasab.

His last meeting with his brother Suleiman on 29 July evening was a poignant one. Yakub expressed his concern for his family and asked his brother to take care of his wife and daughter, Zubaida.

Suleiman and Yakub's cousin Usman took the body, which was flown to Mumbai and buried by his family members, friends and mourners. Huge crowds had gathered to witness the burial. More than 7500 policemen, 125 Rapid Action Force (RAF) personnel and riot control police were deployed at Mahim and other places in Mumbai.

According to media reports, the Memons had raised two requests. One was to ease security and allow them to hold *namaz-e-janaaza* (funeral prayers) on the streets of Mahim. Their second request, which was to allow them to see Yakub's face for the last time, was rejected by police, citing the risk of this creating a law-and-order situation.

Even as the execution of the terrorist convicted for the Mumbai blasts became imminent, renewed demands for abolishing the institution of the death penalty were heard.

While activist lawyers questioned the judicial process and raised doubts about the procedures followed in Yakub's case by the apex court, about three hundred prominent citizens, including eight retired judges of the Supreme Court and the Delhi High Court, urged the President to commute Yakub's sentence to life imprisonment, reflecting what appears to be a growing uneasiness in India with the death penalty. They were also critical of Yakub's hanging.

The All India Majlis-e-Ittehadul Muslimeen chief Asaduddin Owaisi, and few other Muslim bodies, even went to the extent of saying that Yakub was being targeted because he was a Muslim.

The international voices against Yakub's hanging were

led by UN Secretary General Ban Ki-moon. Even the New York–based NGO Human Rights Watch urged India to ban it, saying there is no evidence that the 'cruel' punishment acts as a deterrent.

Prominent opposition leaders too joined activists in calling for a ban; the government responded by saying it could not afford to take the leap just then. The chorus was led by Congress leader Shashi Tharoor who said that 'state-sponsored killing' reduces citizens to murderers. 'There is no evidence that the death penalty serves as a deterrent: to the contrary in fact. All it does is exact retribution: unworthy of a government,' Tharoor tweeted, though he didn't comment on the merits of the Yakub sentence.

The Congress party welcomed the hanging, while Left parties reiterated their stand against capital punishment. Union minister Arun Jaitley called the debate 'legitimate', but made it clear that there was no way India could afford to take the leap at that time due to concerns over internal security and cross-border terrorism.

This was when Yakub was given a patient hearing all through. He was allowed to get the benefit of the due process of law and exhaust all his options before he was hanged, despite there being incriminating circumstantial evidence against him, as pointed out by the well-reasoned court orders, which stated that Yakub Razak Memon was guilty and that terror can never be justified.

The real travesty is that it took the judicial system over two decades to decide his case. India has not yet been able to bring to justice any of the key perpetrators of the 1993 bombings. The prime conspirators are still at large. In spite of credible evidence against Dawood Ibrahim and Tiger Memon, India's efforts to get them extradited have yielded no result.

A large section of the media felt that this was time for India to rethink the capital punishment laws. 'India's use of the death penalty demeans the most cherished idea on which our republic rests, the idea of justice,' wrote the *Indian Express* in its editorial.[4] 'A truly lasting solution to the moral dilemma that each instance of capital punishment poses will be to abolish it altogether and replace it with a sentence of imprisonment for the rest of the convict's life,' wrote *The Hindu*.[5]

More than 160 countries have abolished the death penalty in law or in practice and ninety-eight of those have abolished it altogether. India is one of the fifty-eight countries that still hand out the death penalty, according to a UN report.

Arguments made in favour of the deterrent effects of the death penalty have been proved to be empty, as it is quite rare and only given to those who commit exceptionally brutal or gruesome acts, where pardon is unthinkable.

Courts in India had awarded the death penalty to 2052 convicts between 1998 and 2013, according to the National Crime Records Bureau (NCRB), but only four executions have taken place so far. Others such as R. Jagannathan, the then editor-in-chief at *Firstpost* argued in favour of retaining the maximum penalty, saying that it may be possible to abolish it in extremely advanced countries where people are normally law-abiding and the state is strong enough and has enough resources to even attempt to correct the behaviour patterns of deadly criminals. 'But India is not anywhere near that stage . . . We need the death penalty for our own reasons at this stage in our development as a civilised society,' he wrote in his column. He further stated:

> The right to life is the most fundamental of rights. No state should be allowed to take it away easily. But no fundamental right is without riders either. Free speech, property and faith, all these are rights subject to reasonable restrictions. Sure, the right to life is even more fundamental, but this only means that the right to take it away has to be foolproof and not amenable to subjective readings . . .
>
> When someone is a terrorist, killing people at will, or a serial murderer or rapist, is this person's right to life all that sacrosanct all the time?[6]

The debate over the death penalty has been ongoing for many years. It's a constant source of controversy. The general feeling is that there is no credible evidence that the death penalty deters crime more effectively than a prison term. The government often resorts to the death penalty, using it as a plea to safeguard 'national security'. The questions remains— will the threat of execution stop people who are prepared to die for their beliefs?

Amnesty International is against the death penalty; it considers it a violation of the most fundamental human right—the right to life. Our reverence and respect to the fundamental right to life ushers in one of the most basic thought processes: Should the power of retribution be allowed to prevail over the scope for rehabilitation? It is important to bear in mind that the end is inevitable . . . the divine justice.

10

The Transgender Agenda

Forging a New Identity

'To those who are gay, lesbian, bisexual, or transgender, let me say: you are not alone. Your struggle for the end to violence and discrimination is a shared struggle . . . Today, I stand with you, and I call upon all countries and people to stand with you, too.

A historic shift is underway . . . We must tackle the violence, decriminalize consensual same-sex relationships, ban discrimination and educate the public. I count on this council and people of conscience to make this happen. The time has come.'

—Ban Ki-moon

Mumbai-based Madhuri Sarode, who was born as Prakash, a male, was often thrashed by her parents and her two elder siblings for being effeminate as she liked to dance wearing her sisters' frocks. She bagged top prizes in Kathak competitions in school and in neighbourhood functions. 'My parents were happy about my talent, but they didn't like that I won prizes while dancing as a girl. I was often teased in college for dressing up like a "lady boy" in male clothes with long hair. I always feared being sexually abused . . .

'Despite that, I chose to stay at home with my family as I didn't want to land up begging on streets or forced into sex work as other transgenders. I didn't want that for myself,' she said. Even living at home had become difficult as communication within the family was totally severed. The family insisted that Sarode should abandon this life, but she couldn't live as a male.[1]

The story of another such person, whose name has not been disclosed, is no different:

> Ever since I can remember, I have always identified myself as a woman. I lived in Namakkal, a small town in Tamil Nadu. When I was in the 10th standard I realised that the only way for me to be comfortable was to join the hijra community. It was then that my family found out that I frequently met hijras who lived in the city. One day, when my father was away, my brother, encouraged by my mother, started beating me with a cricket bat. I locked myself in a room to escape from the beatings. My mother and brother then tried to break into the room to beat me up further. Some of my relatives intervened and brought me out of the room. I related my ordeal to an uncle of mine who gave me Rs 50 and asked me to go home. Instead, I took the money and went to live with a group of hijras in Erode.

Then there's Laxmi, who has embraced her identity despite all odds:

Growing up as a child, I felt different from the boys of my age and was feminine in my ways. On account of my femininity, from an early age, I faced repeated sexual harassment, molestation and sexual abuse, both within and outside the family. Due to my being different, I was isolated and had no one to talk to or express my feelings while I was coming to terms with my identity. I was constantly abused by everyone as a 'chakka' and 'hijra'. Though I felt that there was no place for me in society, I did not succumb to the prejudice. I started to dress and appear in public in women's clothing in my late teens but I did not identify as a woman. Later, I joined the Hijra community in Mumbai as I identified with the other hijras and for the first time in my life, I felt at home.

Sachin, a twenty-three-year-old transgender person, has battled with prejudice since childhood:

As a child I always enjoyed putting make-up like 'vibhuti' or 'kum kum' and my parents always saw me as a girl. I am male but I only have female feelings. I used to help my mother in all the housework like cooking, washing and cleaning. Over the years I started assuming more of the domestic responsibilities at home. The neighbours started teasing me. They would call out to me and ask: 'Why don't you go out and work like a man?' or 'Why are you staying at home like a girl?' But I liked being a girl. I felt shy about going out and working. Relatives would also mock and scold me on this score. Every day I would go out of the house to bring water. And as I walked back with the water I would always be teased. I felt very ashamed. I even felt suicidal.

How could I live like that? But my parents never protested. They were helpless.

These are just some of the stories which were discussed in the case before the Supreme Court. The Supreme Court bench made the following observations in the judgment:

Transgender (TG) is generally described as an umbrella term for persons whose gender identity, gender expression or behaviour does not conform to their biological sex. TG also takes in persons who do not identify with their sex assigned at birth, which include Hijras or Eunuchs who describe themselves as 'third gender' and they do not identify as either male or female. Hijras are not men by virtue of anatomy appearance and psychologically, they are also not women, though they are like women with no female reproduction organ and no menstruation. Since Hijras do not have reproduction capacities as either men or women, they are neither men nor women and claim to be an institutional 'third gender'.

TG also includes persons who intend to undergo Sex Re-Assignment Surgery (SRS) or have undergone SRS to align their biological sex with their gender identity in order to become male or female. They are generally called transsexual persons. Further, there are persons who like to cross-dress in clothing of opposite gender, i.e. transvestites. Resultantly, the term 'transgender', in contemporary usage, has become an umbrella term that is used to describe a wide range of identities and experiences, including but not limited to pre-operative, post-operative and non-operative transsexual people, who strongly identify with the gender opposite to their biological sex; male and female.

Etymologically, the term 'transgender' is derived from two words, namely 'trans' and 'gender'. The former is a Latin word which means 'across' or 'beyond'.

In the Indian context, the TG community has a strong historical presence across Hindu mythology, and other religious texts. The concept of *tritiyaprakrti* or *napunsaka* has also been an integral part of Vedic and Puranic literature. The word *napunsaka* has been used to denote absence of procreative capability.

In the Hindu mythology, Lord Rama, in the epic Ramayana, when leaving for the forest upon being banished from the kingdom for 14 years, asks all the men and women to return to the city. Among his followers, the hijras alone do not feel bound by this direction and decide to stay with him. Impressed with their devotion, Rama sanctions them the power to confer blessings on people on auspicious occasions like childbirth and marriage, and also at inaugural functions, which it is believed set the stage for the custom of *badhai* in which hijras sing, dance and confer blessings.

Hijras also had a prominent role to play in the royal courts of the Islamic world, especially in the Ottoman empires and the Mughal kingdoms of medieval India. However, things changed during the British rule. A legislation called the Criminal Tribes Act was enacted in 1871, which deemed the entire community of hijras as innately 'criminal'. Under the Act, the local government had to register the names and residence of all eunuchs residing in that area as well as of their properties. At the time, the community was suspected of kidnapping and castrating children, or of committing offences under Section 377 of the IPC. The provision, which came into force in 1862, defines unnatural offences. It says, 'Whoever voluntarily has carnal intercourse against the order of nature with any man, woman or animal, shall be punished with imprisonment for life, or with imprisonment of either description for a term which may extend to 10 years, and shall also be liable to fine.'

The Act was repealed in August 1949, but the discrimination against transgender persons persists. Transgender persons or eunuchs or hijras, as they are usually referred to, are ostracized, humiliated and sneered at during every stage of life. Their life becomes a challenge the moment they are born. Fear, shame, homelessness, depression and discrimination tend to leave social scars for many of the members of the community. They often face immense physical, emotional and sexual abuse both at home and school. Emotional violence is the most traumatic, besides physical and sexual violence. Many gender-non-conforming children drop out of school due to harassment and discrimination. Without education and jobs, many transgender persons or transwomen (men who express themselves as women) take to sex work. They are often used by men for sex, only to be abandoned later. Marriages generally end in separation due to societal pressures.

After they enter the community of hijras, they are generally abandoned by their families or they become runaways at an early age. Tobacco and alcohol abuse, lack of medical facilities and other basic rights, and issues related to marriage and adoption are problems that they face all through their lives.

And if that were not enough, they also have to live with extortion and violence at the hands of the police all the time.

The community forces them to enter the *jamaat* or 'guru-chela', an order where they get shelter and earn a livelihood, usually by begging and/or sex work, and the guru gets a commission on their earnings.

In spite of the adoption of the Universal Declaration of Human Rights (UDHR) in the year 1948, which upholds the inherent dignity, equality, respect and rights of all human beings throughout the world, transgender persons are denied basic human rights. Our society often ridicules and abuses them, especially in public places, without realizing the trauma, agony and pain which they undergo.

The Case for Equal Rights for Everyone

The National Legal Services Authority (NALSA) believed that the Indian TG community were denied their basic human rights. Hence it decided to knock on the doors of the Supreme Court in 2012 to grant equal rights and protection to them. This mainly included bringing in a 'third gender' category, which was distinct from 'male' and 'female', in identity documents like the election card, passport, driver's licence and ration card. It also included revising the terms of eligibility for transgender persons seeking admissions to educational institutions and hospitals, amongst others.

NALSA was set up in 1997 to provide free legal services to the weaker and marginalized sections of the society. The central argument raised by them was that it was the non-recognition of their gender identity that violated the transgender people's right to equality, equal protection of law and the right to life and personal liberty guaranteed by the Constitution.[2] These fundamental rights and privileges entitle them to the basic necessities of life, including nutrition, shelter, medical facilities, education, the right to work, vote and contest elections as natural persons, NALSA's senior lawyer Raju Ramachandran argued.

The authority also found support from the Lawyers Collective, which moved an intervention application on behalf of Laxmi Narayan Tripathi, a transgender activist from Mumbai. She sought the recognition of the self-identified gender of persons, either as male/female/third gender, based on their choice. Laxmi through senior lawyer Anand Grover (also project director of the HIV/AIDS unit of the Lawyers Collective in Delhi) asserted that fundamental rights guaranteed to every citizen would inevitably include transgender persons. Thus these rights could not be denied or taken away because of their sexual orientation or because they did not have the developed genitalia of a certain gender.

The substance of their argument was that the transgender community has a legal right to decide their sexual orientation and to espouse and determine their identity.

Highlighting the traumatic experiences of the community, Ramachandran also apprised the court of the restricted access the community has to education, healthcare and public places. And their predicament is no better than any outcast or untouchable.

Ramachandran felt that 'the right to choose one's gender identity is integral to the right to lead a life with dignity, which is guaranteed by the Constitution of India'.[3] He reiterated that the problem of the transgender community is a sensitive human issue which called for serious attention. Grover agreed with Ramachandran while tracing the historical background of third-gender identity in India and the position accorded to them in Hindu mythology, as well as Vedic and Puranic literatures. As mentioned earlier, they had also played a prominent role in the royal courts of the Islamic world.

The government refused to acknowledge them as a separate or backward class for reservation in jobs by submitting that 'the existing schemes for OBCs [other backward classes] do not specifically mention transgenders'.

'Transgenders are not denied rights like food, shelter and marriage,' the Ministry of Social Justice and Empowerment stated in its affidavit. The government, represented by Additional Solicitor General Rakesh K. Khanna, maintained that transgender persons and eunuchs were eligible to be enrolled as voters and the Election Commission of India had already issued directions relating to their enrolment, by providing the 'Other' option in the gender column of official documentation. Further, the commission had directed the chief electoral officers of all states/Union Territories to make necessary modifications in the electoral rolls, the government's affidavit pointed out.

The government also argued that during population enumeration, three codes were provided: Male-1, Female-2 and Others-3. 'In case anyone wished to be recorded neither 1 nor 2, then the enumerator was to record their sex under "others" during census,' the ministry had stressed.

The Third Gender

A path-breaking achievement in the struggle for transgender rights came on 15 April 2014, when the Supreme Court delivered a judgment granting legal recognition to transgenders as the 'third gender' as a mandate of social justice, which aims at the breaking of barriers for social mobility, the creation of safety nets and economic justice. The concept of social justice has often referred to the process of ensuring that individuals fulfil their societal roles and receive their due from the society. The historic judgment stated:

> The Constitution has fulfilled its duty of providing rights to transgenders. Now it is time for us to recognise this and to extend and interpret the Constitution in such a manner to ensure a dignified life [for] transgender people. All this can be achieved if the beginning is made with the recognition [of] TGs as third gender.

The bench comprising justices K.S. Radhakrishnan and A.K. Sikri in separate but concurring judgments asked the Centre and the states to recognize transgender persons as a class apart from male and female since they had a right to choose their gender based on the self-identification of their sex. One's right to self-identify one's sex is a facet of the basic principle of dignity, the bench noted, adding that the identification of transgender persons did not require a statutory regime and that their rights were inherent in the Indian Constitution. It said that a 'human rights approach was required to change the social stigma attached to them'.

The important part of the decision was that identification as the third gender required the application of a psychological and not biological test. The bench ruled that:

> Recognition of transgenders as a third gender is not a social or medical issue, but a human rights issue ... Transgenders are also citizens of India. It is the right of every human being to choose their gender. The spirit of the Constitution is to provide equal opportunity to every citizen to grow and attain their potential, irrespective of caste, religion or gender.

The judgment recognized that the gender identity of a person is not necessarily determined biologically and self-identification is an important aspect of gender identity. Every person has the right to determine how they are perceived by the society.

Besides, it attributed to them socially and economically backward status, thus entitling them to reservations under the OBC quota, similar to the ones held for other minority groups in India. Alongside this recognition, the court ordered the Centre and state governments to frame various social welfare and educational schemes for their upliftment and provide quotas across jobs and education.

The judgment was restricted to 'transgender' persons, and explicitly excluded lesbians, gays and bisexuals, thereby not going into the controversial question of the validity of Section 377 of the IPC. Both people who want to transition from their respective genders and the ones who want to be identified with the third gender were included within the ambit of the judgment.

The verdict also directed the Centre and state governments to provide separate HIV Sero-surveillance Centres, medical care and other facilities. Social welfare schemes for their betterment and for creating public awareness too are to be initiated.

An expert committee under the Ministry of Social Justice and Empowerment was set up to conduct an in-depth study of the problems related to transgender persons. The committee was to recommend and adopt measures that would help them regain the respect and place they once enjoyed in our cultural and social life.

While recognizing the third gender, the court based its reasoning on constitutional principles and fundamental rights. It pointed out that the Indian Constitution is not gender-specific and fundamental rights are guaranteed to every Indian citizen irrespective of their gender. It declared that the term 'person' in the Constitution also includes 'transgender'.

On a sensitive note, Justice Radhakrishnan shared:

Seldom, our society realizes or cares to realize the trauma, agony and pain which the members of transgender community undergo, nor appreciates the innate feelings of the members of the transgender community, especially of those whose mind and body disown their biological sex. Our society often ridicules and abuses the transgender community, and in public places like railway stations, bus stands, schools, workplaces, malls, theatres, hospitals, they are sidelined and treated as untouchables.

The discrimination on the basis of sexual orientation

or gender identity includes any discrimination, exclusion, restriction or preference, which has the effect of nullifying or transposing equality by the law or the equal protection of laws guaranteed under our Constitution, and hence we are inclined to give various directions to safeguard the constitutional rights of the members of the TG community.

He also asked the government to construct special washrooms and create health departments to take care of transsexual medical needs.

Justice Sikri, another judge on the bench, concurred with Justice Radhakrishnan in his judgment, which was bound to bring a sea change in the lives of transgender persons.

Justice Sikri emphasized that in international human rights law, equality is founded upon two complementary principles: non-discrimination and reasonable differentiation. In a separate ruling, he added:

The principle of non-discrimination seeks to ensure that all persons can equally enjoy and exercise all their rights and freedoms. Discrimination occurs due to arbitrary denial of opportunities for equal participation. For example, when public facilities and services are set on standards out of the reach of the TGs, it leads to exclusion and denial of rights. Equality not only implies preventing discrimination, but goes beyond remedying discrimination against groups suffering systematic discrimination in society. In concrete terms, it means embracing the notion of positive rights, affirmative action and reasonable accommodation.

The Trial

After establishing the stand of transgender persons in India and their plight and predicament, the court proceedings focused on gender identity and sexual orientation.

Gender identity, which refers to a person's intrinsic sense of being male, female or transgender or transsexual, is one of the most fundamental aspects of life. A person's sex is usually assigned at birth, but a relatively small group of people are born with bodies which incorporate both or certain aspects of both male and female physiology. Gender identity refers to one's internal and individual experience of gender. This may or may not correspond with the sex assigned at birth. It includes how one experiences the body—which may involve a freely chosen modification of one's bodily appearance or functions through medical, surgical or other means—and other expressions of gender, including dress, speech and mannerisms.

Sexual orientation refers to a person's enduring physical, romantic and/or emotional attraction to another gender. This includes the orientation of transgender and gender-variant people, which may or may not change during or after gender transmission, and also the orientation of homosexuals, bisexuals, heterosexuals, asexuals, etc. Gender variance refers to behaviours and interests that are not consistent with an individual's gender but are more typical of the opposite sex. For example, a girl who insists on having short hair and prefers to play football with the boys, or a boy who wears frocks and wishes to be a princess, is considered to be exhibiting gender-variant or gender-non-conforming behaviours and interests.

While studying the transgender case, the court made reference to the United Nations and its role in advocating the protection and promotion of the rights of sexual minorities, including the transgender community. In addition, the court considered various international instruments such as the UDHR, 1948, the International Covenant on Civil and Political Rights, 1966, as well as the domestic legislations of other countries. The court also took into account several international conventions and the Yogyakarta Principles—a universal guide to human rights which affirm binding legal international standards which all states must comply with.

In 2006, a distinguished group of international human rights experts met in Yogyakarta, Indonesia, to outline a set of international principles relating to sexual orientation and gender identity. The result was the Yogyakarta Principles, which emphasize that all human beings are born free and equal in terms of dignity and rights. Human beings of all sexual orientations and gender identities are entitled to the full enjoyment of all human rights. The principles also advocate the right to recognition before the law.[4]

Various UN bodies, regional human rights bodies, national courts, government commissions, the Commission on Human Rights and the Council of Europe, among others, have endorsed the Yogyakarta Principles—which address the application of a broad range of human rights standards to issues of sexual orientation and gender identity—and consider them an important tool for identifying the obligations of states to respect, protect and fulfil the human rights of all persons, regardless of their gender identity.

The NALSA judgment has been a big step towards encouraging acceptance and recognition of the transgender community, but a lot more needs to be achieved. Beyond the case is the cause, and beyond the cause is the concern. Justice Sikri and Justice Radhakrishnan did their best; they recommended the establishment of a committee under the Ministry of Social Justice and Empowerment to look into the cause and to implement improvement measures. It is concern that is of paramount importance, the concern of the public, the citizens, that will help change the social environment.

By validating the third gender, the court not only championed the rule of law but also did justice to the community, so far deprived of their legitimate constitutional and natural rights. It is, therefore, a just solution that ensures justice not only for transgender persons but also for society as well.

Adequate infrastructure alone is not enough. A shift in the thought process and societal mindsets, as well as a greater degree of tolerance and acceptance, are required to bring about change.

Another good thing about the NALSA judgment was that it created a heightened awareness about the transgender community. The fact that they are deprived of social and cultural participation and that they have restricted access to education, healthcare and public places has now been brought to the forefront.

The judgment brought relief to an estimated 3 million people within India. It has enabled transgender people to have equal access to education, healthcare and employment, as well as protection from discrimination.

Lawyer Anand Grover feels that the NALSA judgment has paved the way for the Supreme Court to conduct oral hearings and accept the curative petition filed by the Naz Foundation, another NGO, on 22 April 2014. The rationale of reading both gender identity and sexuality into the Constitution formed the basis for reopening the case pertaining to the rights of the LGBT community; the judgment could be an important milestone in furthering the cause against Section 377. The awareness about gender identity and sexual orientation is increasing among people and thus raising the need for accepting difference. The Supreme Court's progressive judgment has been a cornerstone in the project to establish a more diversified and liberal society.

Overcoming Social Stigma

Laxmi Narayan Tripathi or Laxmi, a transgender person, an activist and a spokesperson for the Kinnar community, has been instrumental in initiating the process of bringing about change. Her mission is to provide other transgender people a beautiful life, a life which they deserve. She is also the first transgender person to write her own autobiography.[5] In 2007, Laxmi started an organization called Astitva to promote the welfare of sexual minorities. With this, she led a revolution for people like her from all over the world. She is the first transgender person to represent the Asia-Pacific at the UN in 2008.

A champion of the transgender cause, Laxmi was open about her sexuality, but faced repeated sexual harassment and abuse, both within and outside her family. 'Though I felt that there was no place for me in the society, I did not succumb to the prejudice,' she has said. She dressed in women's clothing in her late teens but did not identify as a woman. Later, when she joined the hijra community, she was relieved and felt at home. 'I was technically a man for people, but deep inside I was aware of my original identity . . . That was the time I learnt to believe in myself and trust my instincts,' says Laxmi, who participated in season 5 of the TV show *Big Boss* and was seen with Salman Khan in *Dus Ka Dum*. She was also featured in the shows *Sach Ka Samna* and *Raaz Pichle Janam Ka*, and has starred in an award-winning documentary in 2005 called *Between the Lines: India's Third Gender*. In 2011, Laxmi starred in *Queens! Destiny of Dance*, an award-winning Bollywood movie about hijras which garnered rave reviews.

Laxmi did her schooling from the Sulochanadevi Singhania School in Thane, acquired an arts degree from Mumbai's Mithibai College and has a postgraduate degree in Bharatanatyam. In 2002, she became the president of the Dai Welfare Society, the first registered and working NGO for eunuchs in South Asia. *Red Lipstick*, her autobiography, is co-authored with Pooja Pande and provides glimpses of her life. She has two adopted children and lives in Mumbai.[6]

Others too have shown exemplary courage post the NALSA judgment. So inspired was Naina, a student of Vasant Valley school, New Delhi, that she came out in the open and bravely declared her sexual identity to teachers and students gathered during a school assembly in 2015. Having grown up as a boy named Krishna, the seventeen-year-old had always liked dressing up in women's clothes, hanging out with girls at family functions and discussing make-up. She had battled suicidal tendencies and depression. But with the support of her mother and close friends, she dared to let the world know her real identity.[7]

On 28 December 2016, Madhuri Sarode, a transgender person, openly tied the knot in a temple ceremony with Jay Rajnath Sharma, a resident of Jaunpur in Uttar Pradesh whom she met on Facebook. Madhuri found an ideal partner in Jay who accepted her sexuality. The wedding ceremony was an elaborate affair: mehendi, haldi and sangeet ceremonies, and the exchange of garlands and *phera*s, followed by a reception for family and friends.[8] As per Madhuri:

> Marriages do take place in the TG (transgender) community, but never openly. It's usually a small affair with a handful of friends, a mere exchange of rings or garlands. But I didn't want that. I wanted to have a proper invitation card, an album of pictures, a wedding outfit like everyone else. If the Supreme Court ruled in 2014 that transgender be recognised as the third sex and given equal rights, then why can I not have all these things?[9]

She now wants to set it as a precedent for the rest of the community and is keen on getting a marriage certificate as a transgender person. 'If the authorities refuse me one, which I am sure they will, I will take the fight to the court. How long can we wait to be treated as equals, as humans?' she asks.

Madhuri had a sex-change surgery in 2011. She continues to identify as a transgender person and hopes to continue battling for the community's rights. 'I can get a marriage certificate as a woman. It won't be difficult. But why should

I have to do that?' she asks. Born as Prakash, a male, Madhuri joined the NGO Humsafar Trust as a volunteer. 'I was a huge fan of Madhuri Dixit, a famous Bollywood actress. People used to call me "Madhuri Dixit of the TG community". No performance [dance] of mine even today is complete without her song.' That's how Prakash came to be called Madhuri.

Within the third-gender community, there are many exceptional examples of how members did not let societal pressure decide their fate. In the last two decades, there have been some groundbreaking milestones in their journey. Shabnam 'Mausi' Bano became the first Indian transwoman to be elected as a member of a state Legislative Assembly (Madhya Pradesh), serving from 1998 to 2003. Madhu Bai Kinnar, a street-play artist and also a folk-dance performer, became the first transgender mayor of the Raigarh district in Chhattisgarh.

This was not the first time India has elected a transgender mayor. Madhya Pradesh has elected transgender persons to office twice. Kamla Jaan was elected mayor of Katni in 1999 and Kamla Kinnar of Sagar in 2009. But their elections were declared null and void by courts and they had to step down from the post as the seats were reserved for women.

Kalki Subramaniam was one of the first noted transgender entrepreneurs. She is also a writer, actor and activist. She is the founder of the Sahodari Foundation, which works for the upliftment of the transgender community. Padmini Prakash, a vocal artist, trained Indian classical dancer and Miss Transgender of India, read out her first headline bulletin at Coimbatore-based Lotus News Channel on

TV, thus becoming the first transgender news anchor in India. Manabi Bandyopadhyay, author of a bestselling novel *Endless Bondage* about hijras, became the country's first trans principal of a women's college in West Bengal on 9 June 2015. Manabi, whose earlier name was Somnath, underwent a series of operations in 2003–04 and became a woman. In 1995, she published the country's first transgender magazine, *Ob-Manab* (Sub-human). Her biography, *A Gift of Goddess Lakshmi*, was published in February 2017. Then there is the indomitable Abhina Aher, a transgender activist and national programme manager with the India HIV/AIDS Alliance, who has been working on sexuality, gender, health and human rights issues for almost two decades.

The Changing Scenario

Anjali Lama created a huge flutter in the fashion industry when she became the first transgender model to walk the ramp. Lama was booked for more than a dozen runway shows during the Lakme Fashion Week held in Mumbai in February 2017 where she walked alongside Bollywood stars and celebrities like Padma Lakshmi.[10]

'Life is what we make of it and the walls we erect to segregate or discriminate are reflective of the big walls in our own minds,' said veteran designer Tarun Tahiliani, adding that no one had the right to strip anyone's self-respect and that everyone should be given a fair chance to make a livelihood. Amit Aggarwal, one of the designers who cast her, said that he didn't know Lama was a transgender person, but cast her for his show 'because I loved her . . . it was a proud moment for me to see her wear my clothes. It expanded the language of my own creativity.'

The state governments too are doing their bit to create awareness and uplift the community.

A mega sports meet for transgender people, the first of its sort in the country, was held in Kerala in April 2017 with at least 130 transgender athletes participating in the event. It was a 'runaway hit. We are really bowled over by the cheers and encouragement of the audience. Hundreds turned up to witness it. It really shows society is gradually changing their attitude towards the sexual minority,' said Sreekutty, president of the Sexual and Gender Minority, an organization that focuses on the third sex.

Transgender rights activist Kalki Subramaniam inaugurated the Sahaj International School in December 2016. It is a residential school for transgender persons in Kochi to help adults who drop out of school to finish their education. It promotes inclusive education, and offers free sex reassignment surgery or SRS at government hospitals.

'The school aims at making transgenders eligible for taking decent jobs and living a dignified life,' says transgender activist Vijayraja Mallika, who heads the school.

The government has now allowed members of the community to use the toilets of their choice. The Ministry of Drinking Water and Sanitation issued guidelines to the Swachh Bharat Mission (Gramin) stating that members of the third-gender community should be allowed to use the public toilets of their choice, whether those meant for men or women.

Dhananjay Chauhan, a transgender activist, was successful

in his struggle to have a separate toilet established for transgender persons in Panjab University.

Procter & Gamble's cough and cold brand Vicks's new ad in 2017—'Touch of Care'—reveals the human side of the transgender issue. The three-and-a-half-minute-long emotive ad has become quite popular on social media and has been acclaimed for featuring the true story of Gayatri, an orphan who found a loving mother—a thirty-seven-year-old Mumbai-based transgender activist Gauri Sawant.[11]

The campaign shows how people who, though not connected by blood, end up being family by caring for each other. The Vicks advertisement is a small step towards stirring debate on this issue and bringing it to a wider audience. To adopt or to have a child should go beyond one's gender or sexuality. Gauri Sawant's life story is a model for society. Transgender people—along with same-sex couples—still cannot legally adopt children in India. Though the Supreme Court recognized the constitutional right of transgenders, the Indian adoption laws still don't give a transman or transwoman the right to legally adopt a child.

At the workplace, equality still continues to be a distant dream for them. 'Corporate jobs are a sign that society has accepted them. It helps break certain stereotypes about them, and gives them a certain degree of respect,' said Anupama Easwaran, founder, in.harmony, a diversity and inclusion consultancy.

In 2014, Udupi became the first transgender employee to work at ThoughtWorks India. 'It is important for companies to consider us,' said Anvesha B., a transgender person. 'If the message is out that employers are giving us a chance, transgender people wouldn't have to take to sex work and begging,' said the twenty-five-year-old, who is an engineer by qualification.[12]

The Indian Railway Catering and Tourism Corporation (IRCTC) has also introduced 'transgender' as the third option besides 'male' and 'female' in ticket reservation and cancellation forms. The move follows a petition filed by Delhi-based lawyer Jamshed Ansari, who had also asked for special coaches and reserved seats in all trains for members of the transgender community.

In March 2015, those filling the online passport application form had the option of choosing 'transgender' apart from 'male' or 'female' in the gender category. Aimed at encouraging members of the community to open bank accounts, the Reserve Bank of India in April 2015 directed banks to include a 'third gender' option in all their forms and applications.

Recognition and acceptance is a long-drawn process in our society. What gets acceptance on paper does not necessarily get acceptance in life. The level of tolerance has no measure and is often subjective, impenetrable and unpredictable.

In June 2014, a transgender person died following an accident, as doctors could not decide which ward—male or female—to use for treatment. In February 2015, the Telangana Hijra Transgender Samiti reported forty attacks on transgender people within a six-month period. Many similarly disheartening incidents have occurred post the NALSA judgment and may continue for some more time.[13] Change has its own pace.

While the NALSA judgment asked the government to

design affirmative action policies for the community, little has been done on the implementation front. After a promising 2015 draft bill, the Transgender Persons (Protection of Rights) Bill, 2016, in fact, undid a lot of what the apex court tried to do. In August 2016, the Central government introduced the bill in Lok Sabha. It sought to define the term 'transgender' and prohibit discrimination against the community.

Activists have criticized the 2016 draft bill as undermining the Supreme Court's 2014 ruling. The critique issued by the NGO Sampoorna held that the 2015 version of the draft bill honoured the right of transgender people to self-determine their gender identity and reiterated that transgender identity is not dependent on any medical or surgical intervention.

The 2016 bill provided for the right to perceived gender identity and also made it mandatory for such transgender persons to apply to a district screening committee, comprising the chief medical officer (CMO), the district social welfare officer, a psychologist or psychiatrist, a representative of the transgender community and an officer of the relevant government.

The committee would conduct an inquiry and 'certify' transgender identities for applicants. That a supra-constitutional body will determine the identity of transgender people is a gross violation of human rights and constitutional principles. Involving a CMO for screening also means that members of the third gender would be subject to arbitrary medical examinations and allied humiliation and that this would be sanctioned by the state, activists argued.

A mixed reaction prevails in the community today.

The community feels that the state machinery is slow and victimization persists. 'Passing a law doesn't change society overnight . . . the government, the public, the activists need to work together to promote transgender rights and equality,' said the actress, artist and transgender rights activist Kalki Subramaniam.

While India's transgender rights movement has made significant progress in recent years, the community continues to face widespread discrimination and challenges in society. Abhina Aher explained that things have moved very slowly:

> We are still struggling for basic things. As for employment in the private sector, transpeople are facing a Catch-22 situation, where employers are perhaps not ostensibly transphobic, but expect qualifications and experience that most don't have access to. I think there should be a specific skill development programme for transpeople as well. Economic disempowerment and residential issues are also a huge concern.[14]

A lot has changed, but there is a long way to go.

11

The Bar Dancers Case

A Morality Play

'Our moods and insights are transitory. This current is a flow of grace moving us to our right livelihood, companions, destiny.'

—Julia Cameron

Sixteen-year-old Tarannum Khan's home was burnt down in the Mumbai communal riots that took place after the demolition of the Babri Masjid in December 1992. Her house was ransacked and destroyed. She found herself on the streets with her parents and siblings . . . They had become homeless. After a temporary stay at a relief camp in Milat Nagar, Andheri, in Mumbai, the family was again out on the streets of Lokhandwala. For three nights, they went without food and shelter.[1]

A recent surgery had made her father weak and it was difficult for him to go out to work. Her mother was willing to do anything for money. Survival had become difficult.

Tarannum had just finished her twelfth class and finding a job was not easy. The pressing circumstances made her accept a bar dancer's job; she wanted to earn a livelihood to feed her family. In her statement to the income tax department, Tarannum explained how she was initiated into the profession:

> A female approached us, saying that I could earn money by joining a dance bar. For a pious Muslim family like mine, the mere suggestion was blasphemy. But I had only been educated till Std XII, and no one with such a qualification can earn decently to shoulder the responsibility of an entire family. I was 16 but I was ready to do anything to provide a roof over our heads. So, reluctantly, my parents agreed.
>
> The first day of my life in this profession is one which I don't want to remember. Anyway, I started making money, and after a year, I joined Deepa bar and my life turned into a fairytale.
>
> I used to come home at 6 in the morning, eat and go to sleep at 7 am, then get up at 4 in the afternoon and get ready to go to the bar, where I was on my toes for 14 hours every day.[2]

This was just the beginning for the *crorepati* [millionaire] bar dancer. She never wanted to join the disreputable profession and dance in front of inebriated men, but she continued as the money kept coming in.

Deepa Bar in Vile Parle (West) changed her life. The 8000-square-feet property was frequented by the rich and famous: Bollywood celebrities, cricketers, businessmen and politicians. For Tarannum, accepting showers of money and gifts became a routine affair. She had become a sort of celebrity at Deepa Bar.

Over time, Tarannum made so much money through the profession that she earned the nickname of the crorepati bar dancer. With most of her earnings coming from undisclosed sources, her home was raided by the income tax department around 2004–05. She was accused of running a cricket-betting racket.

The dance bars in Mumbai were a flourishing business back then and were often referred to as the jewel in the crown of Mumbai's nightlife. The bar owners would make huge profits as the place was thronged with businessmen, politicians, writers and poets as well. Everyone made money: the bouncers, make-up men, waiters, the autorickshaw drivers—and even the cops, who came in as free customers.

Dance bars originated in and around Mumbai in the 1980s. The culture of dance bars started in Khalapur, in the Raigad district, around 75 km from Mumbai, in the early 1980s. Baywatch was one of the first bars in the area; it functioned quietly at night. Around 500–600 dancers and bar girls were brought from different parts of Mumbai and Thane in buses to the venue in the late afternoon to dance at night. The move soon picked up and spread like wildfire in Mumbai and Thane. At one point of time, there were an estimated 3000 night bars of this kind, employing over 75,000 dancers. Bollywood film-maker Madhur Bhandarkar's 2001 movie *Chandni Bar*, starring actress Tabu, put the spotlight on these dance bars and the people who work there.

People from all age groups—mostly youth and wealthy

businessmen, as well as tourists, both domestic and international—enjoyed an 'interactive' session with the dancers by showering them with currency notes. The smell of cigarette smoke and liquor would linger on for hours . . . Though the unwritten rule was not to touch at the Mumbai dance bars, there were instances when such rules were broken in the rooms on the premises.

Then one day things changed. The Maharashtra government imposed a ban on dance bars in August 2005. Thousands of bar dancers lost their jobs. Consequently, some dancers invested in property or petty businesses while others put their booty in bets or gambling for quick gains. The bar girls protested against the ban, shouting slogans alleging bias and discrimination, and demanding a rehabilitation package. Even members of Parliament and actors Sunil Dutt and Govinda came to their support, and expressed concern over the future of these 75,000 girls who were rendered jobless as a result of the ban.

Initially, the then deputy chief minister R.R. Patil had proposed rehabilitating them, but later he backtracked on this since 75 per cent of the bar girls were from other states, and others from neighbouring Bangladesh. He then suggested that only Maharashtrian girls would be rehabilitated, but finally nothing came of it.

The lack of rehabilitation programmes forced hundreds of bar girls to move to the Gulf and South East Asian countries for sustenance. Thousands were left vulnerable and pushed into sex trafficking. According to Varsha Kale, president of the Bar Girls Association, who has been fighting for out-of-work bar girls, 'Pimps were selling them to other countries because they had no work, no income to feed their families.'[3] In many cases, unemployed girls moved to outright sex work in Mumbai's red-light districts like Kamathipura. The 2005 ban also made them victims of sexual violence, which led to suicide in several cases. The dance bars themselves had to make ends meet by hosting live singing troupes or live bands.

The Background

In 1986, orchestra and dance performances were permitted in hotels. However, violation of the terms and conditions of performance licences under the Bombay Police Act, 1951, was rampant and several cases were registered. Around 20,196 cases were registered between 2000 and 2005. Many cases of minor girls being rescued from dance bars by the Mumbai Police in 2002–05 under the Immoral Traffic (Prevention) Act, 1956, came to light. People had also complained about sex-work rackets being run through pick-up points in the hotels where dance programmes were being conducted. The dance forms presented in these bars were found to be obscene and criminals were allegedly being sheltered in such hotels.

The government was convinced that the obscene dancing and undesirable practices were having an adverse effect on society. In July 2004, an expert committee, which was set up to check undesirable practices going on in dance bars, had suggested various measures, including restrictions on attire, registration of bar girls and the routing of tips/reward money through establishments. In August 2004, the chairperson of the Maharashtra State Commission for Women wrote to the state government about the increasing number of sex rackets and cases of immoral trafficking that were exploiting and forcing bar dancers into sex work, thus 'leading to [the] total destruction of their life'. The letter had further warned the government that the problem in 'all probability would spoil our social health by acquiring increasingly grave dimensions, not confined only to Mumbai but extending to the national and even international levels'. The women's commission also went on to recommend the closure of such establishments.

The state government too felt that the performance of dances in eating houses, permit rooms or beer bars in an indecent manner is derogatory to the dignity of women and is likely to deprave, corrupt and injure public morality. So, in the interest of the general public, the government made a conscious decision to amend the Bombay Police Act, 1951, and added Sections 33(A) and 33(B) to it, thus imposing curbs only on the owners of the prohibited establishments (bars and restaurants with less than a three-star rating) from conducting dance performances. The amended Act was passed by the Maharashtra Legislative Assembly on 14 July 2005 and came into force on 14 August 2005.

———

The termination of these dance performances in bars was challenged by various associations representing restaurants and bars, bar dancers, women's help groups and NGOs working in the field, etc. Apart from raising the issue of the state government's legislative competence to enact the impugned law, as 'morality' does not fall within its ambit, they alleged gender discrimination and infringement of the right to freedom of profession and right to life, which includes the right to livelihood under Article 21 of the Constitution.

The ban, enforced by the Maharashtra government, was struck down by the Bombay High Court in April 2006 as arbitrary and unconstitutional. It slammed the state government for its double standards in allowing bar girls to dance in high-end establishments and at independent performances, while banning them elsewhere.[4]

The government took the matter to the Supreme Court in May 2006 and obtained a stay. The government said that such bars fuelled trafficking, prostitution and the exploitation of women. It also said bar dancing was vulgar and depraved.

On 16 July 2013, the Supreme Court came to the rescue of the dance bars and struck down the Maharashtra government's decision to ban dance by girls in bars and restaurants with less than a three-star rating, saying that the prohibition violated the right to carry on one's profession in a non-discriminatory manner.

A bench comprising the late chief justice Altamas Kabir and Justice S.S. Nijjar upheld the right of women bar dancers to follow their profession while concurring with the views of the high court that the ban was constitutionally impermissible, for prohibiting dances in certain establishments while permitting them in others infringed on the right to equality under Article 14 of the Constitution.

Writing for the bench, Justice Nijjar said in the judgment:

There is no justification that a dance permitted in exempted institutions under Section 33B, if permitted in the banned establishment, would be derogatory, exploitative or corrupting of public morality. We are of the firm opinion that the distinction, the foundation of which are classes of the establishments and classes/kind of persons, who frequent the establishment and those who own the establishments, cannot be supported under the constitutional philosophy so clearly stated in the Preamble of the Constitution and the individual Articles prohibiting discrimination on the basis of caste, colour, creed, religion or gender.

The apex court further said:

Rather it is evident that the same dancer can perform the same dance in the high class hotels, clubs and gymkhanas but is prohibited from doing so in the establishments covered under Section 33A. We see no rationale which would justify the conclusion that a dance that leads to depravity in one place would get converted to an acceptable performance by a mere change of venue. In our opinion, in the present case, the legislation is based on an unacceptable presumption that the so-called elite i.e. the rich and the famous would have higher standards of decency, morality or strength of character than their counterparts who have to content themselves with lesser facilities of inferior quality in the dance bars.

The top court stated that such a presumption is abhorrent to the resolve in the Preamble to secure the citizens of India.

In our opinion, if a certain kind of dance is sensuous in nature and if it causes sexual arousal in men, it cannot be said to be more in the prohibited establishments and less in the exempted establishments. Sexual arousal and lust in men and women and degree thereof cannot be said to be monopolised by the upper or lower classes. Nor can it be presumed that sexual arousal would generate a different character of behaviour, depending on the social strata of the audience.

The Supreme Court noted that most dance bars had literally closed down since 2005 and had led to the unemployment of over 75,000 women workers. It also recorded that many of them were compelled to take up sex work out of necessity, for the maintenance of their families.

Senior counsel Harish N. Salve, Gopal Subramanium and Shekhar Naphade, who appeared on behalf of the Maharashtra government, had emphasized that the state cannot shut its eyes to the larger social problems arising out of bar dancing which are uncontrolled and impossible to regulate.

Highlighting the unhealthy practice of customers showering money on the dancers during performances in the prohibited establishments, the lawyers said that the girls were drawn into unhealthy competition to create and sustain the sexual interest of the most favoured customers. But such behaviour on the part of customers is absent when the dancers are performing in exempted establishments like gymkhanas and hotels with a rating of three stars or more.

Former attorney general and senior lawyer Mukul Rohatgi, and senior counsels Rajeev Dhawan and Anand Grover argued against the ban. They said that the controversy revolved around the right to earn a livelihood more so than the right of a person to choose the vocation of their choice. Rohatgi argued that the classification of establishments—whether they had a three-star rating or more—was not based on any intelligible differentia and was discriminatory and arbitrary. Also, the classification was based on the presumption that the performance of dance in prohibited establishments having lesser facilities than three-star establishments would be derogatory to the dignity of women. The presumption did not have any factual basis, Rohatgi added.

Restrictions imposed by law must be reasonable and in the interest of the general public and cannot be imposed only in the interest of morality or decency. Further, the amendment was neither supported by any evidence to demonstrate that there was any threat to public order nor was there any material to show that the members of the Indian Hotel and Restaurant Association were indulging in human trafficking or flesh trade, the lawyers contended.

Grover refuted the allegation that dancing in bars was a gateway to prostitution; that it was associated with crime and bred criminality; that the conditions of dance bars were exploitative and dehumanizing. He considered this claim of the state government to be incorrect, exaggerated and overstated. He even cited the NCRB report for 2004–11 saying there was no nexus between dance bars and women trafficking. Instead, he argued, the social evils projected were related to the serving and drinking of alcohol and not dancing.

After the 2013 Verdict

Following the Supreme Court's 2013 decision, the then Congress-led Maharashtra government moved to plug the legal loophole.

Instead of accepting the apex court's order to think of 'imaginative alternative steps' to bring about measures which would 'ensure the safety and improve the working conditions of the persons working as bar girls', the state assembly, on 13 June 2014, passed the Maharashtra Police (Second Amendment) Bill, extending the ban to high-end hotels and private clubs, too. It amended Section 33(A), thereby affecting a total ban on dance bars and dance performances in the state. The bill, passed without a debate, also covered drama theatres, cinema halls, auditoriums, sports clubs and gymkhanas, where entry is restricted only to members.

In September 2014, the Maharashtra state-appointed committee headed by former judge Chandrashekhar Shankar Dharmadhikari recommended a complete ban on bar girls in hotels and restaurants as well as curbs on social media in order to reduce crimes against women. It also recommended an 'improved legislation' more than an ordinance.

The 2014 amendment was again challenged by the Indian Hotel and Restaurant Association and others in the apex court, which criticized the state government's decision to impose a total ban on dance bars and dance performances.

Acknowledging the right of women bar dancers to follow their profession, the Supreme Court, on 15 October 2016, suspended the legal provision banning dance performances in Maharashtra and directed the state government to grant licences to the bar owners without insisting on the prohibitory legislation.

Expressing displeasure over how the state government had re-enacted a similar piece of legislation after the top court had struck down a prohibitory provision in 2013, a bench of justices Dipak Misra and P.C. Pant rejected the Maharashtra government's stand that the two provisions were different and that the 2014 amendment was perfectly valid. 'The difference that is perceptible from the provisions which have been reproduced above are really immaterial,' the bench said.

The bench went on to note that there are situations when the 'legislature steps in to remove the base' of a judgment and to validate a provision after the court has declared the provision as unconstitutional. In some other cases, the legislature brings an amendment whereby the defects pointed out by the court are removed, the judges said.

While asking the state government to grant licences to bar owners, the bench added a caveat that 'no performance of dance shall remotely be expressive of any kind of obscenity in any manner' and that 'the licensing authority can take steps so that the individual dignity of a woman is not affected and there remains no room for any kind of obscenity'. It said that the police and other government bodies have sufficient power to 'safeguard any violation of the dignity of women through obscene dances' and to make sure that such performances do not adversely affect public order.

While the Supreme Court was trying to conclude the issue, the state again introduced the Maharashtra Prohibition of Obscene Dance in Hotels, Restaurants and Bar Rooms and Protection of Dignity of Women Act, 2016, on the pretext of regulating dance performances. The new law proposed stringent rules to operate dance bars, including three years in jail for the bar owner if a bargirl indulges in obscenity, no serving of liquor, a mandatory partition between the hotel and dancing area and compulsory CCTVs in such areas. The Act also made it compulsory for dance bar owners to shut shop by 11.30 p.m., besides barring them from operating within a one-kilometre radius of religious and educational establishments. As per its provision, only people above twenty-one years of age were allowed in bars. The government had also allegedly increased the dance-bar licence fee from Rs 2000 to Rs 2 lakh.

This time, the state justified its action on the pretext that there was no 'art' in the dance performed at dance bars and since the bar girls 'aren't trained artistes, their dance has little value and may become obscene'. The state government's senior counsel Shekhar Naphade argued that bar dancing was vulgar and not an art form that needed to be protected and promoted. He further said that most of the times dance bars indulged in sex rackets or acted as pick-up points for prostitutes, perpetuating the exploitation of women.

However, the hotels associations termed the new Act arbitrary and violative of their right to earn a livelihood through legitimate means. Bar girl unions like the Bharatiya Bargirls Union alleged that the new law condemned their profession and unreasonably interfered with the free choice of expression through dramatic performances and the right of women to practise an occupation of self-expression through such performances. It further claimed that the term 'obscene dance' in the Act had been intentionally kept vague so as to allow the police to harass women performers and achieve the political goal of imposing a complete ban on such performances. As per the bar girls' union argument:

The act of tipping or giving gifts as a token of appreciation has been customary and an integral part of traditional dance culture. This decades-old practice is akin to those performing Mujra, Lavani (traditional Marathi song and dance) or Tamasha (traditional Marathi theatre) where performers earn their living through '*bakshis*' offered by the audience as a token of appreciation of the performances. The said practice is widely prevalent in Maharashtra and across the country. But the Act prohibits such practice contrary to traditionally accepted form of custom, thus failing to recognise that every performance deserves a prize.

Legal experts also said that terms like 'lascivious movements', etc., included in the Act were at best vague and expose the dancer and her establishment to the whims of the authorities itching to crack down on them.

———

As a result of the apex court judgment, dance bars were reopened in Maharashtra, which came as a relief for hundreds of establishments and thousands of women who had lost their jobs. These women had slipped into penury and sex work due to the clampdown by the Maharashtra government in July 2014. The Supreme Court decision upheld the idea that 'dancing is a fundamental right'.

Thousands of bar dancers celebrated the verdict by distributing sweets as it reopened an employment opportunity for them. 'Women would not be forced to do anything wrong if bar dancing resumes,' they claimed, smiling at the thought of resuming their old profession. However, they are still apprehensive that the state government will not allow dance bars to function for political reasons.

The ban on dance bars did more harm than good. The shutdown left dancers vulnerable as it failed to provide alternative means of support and shelter to people engaged in such trades or professions—some of whom were trafficked from different parts of the country and had nowhere to go, no other means to earn a living.

Jibing about the classic case of Indian hypocrisy, lawyer Sunil Fernandes said that when film actresses are paid several million rupees to perform an 'item number' in a Bollywood movie, it is considered high art. When skimpily clad, midriff-baring, cleavage-heaving heroines suggestively thrust their pelvis and whatnot, the law of the land considers it an 'art form' and perfectly legal. You can watch it on screen, of course, at an outrageously high-priced ticket, which includes a neat 'entertainment tax' payable to the government. 'Now imagine the same "item number" or "dance number" is performed by a destitute lady, who probably has young children and old parents to feed, in [a] less than sanitised environment, in front of lascivious men masquerading as patrons, the same state government bans it as being "immoral" "unethical" and "illegal",' he stated.

'This is not only a legal and administrative failure of the state government but a moral defeat too,' said Nationalist Congress Party member and the leader of Opposition in the legislative council, Dhananjay Munde.

The Changing Scenario

The majority of bar dancers are in the business due to economic conditions and not because they like doing it. Bar dancing has helped them come out of impoverishment and provide better living conditions for their families and themselves.

Women worldwide are becoming more and more assertive of their rights and want to be free to make their own choices. It is necessary to work towards a change in the mindset of people in general not only by way of laws and other forms of regulations, but also by way of providing suitable amenities for those who want to get out of this profession and to either improve their existing conditions or to begin a new life altogether.

The job of the government is governance, not moral or theological policing. It needs to recognize the right of a woman to earn a living in a manner of her choosing. While the government is responsible for their skill-building, to ensure that no one performs in dance bars due to economic stress, it cannot ban women from earning money from dancing if they so choose to, and that too on the pretext of exploitation.

Senior lawyer Anand Grover said that the impugned law violated the principle of proportionality, adding that:

Gender stereotyping was also palpable in the solution crafted by the legislature. The impugned statute does not affect a man's freedom to visit bars and consume alcohol, but restricted a woman from choosing the occupation of dancing in the same bars. The legislation, patronizingly, seeks to 'protect' women by constraining their liberty, autonomy and self-determination.

There is a need to regulate the dance bars, but not in a way that punishes women. Their rights must be recognized; they cannot be denied the right to choose their profession on the vague and subjective grounds of 'obscenity' and 'immorality'.

While appreciating how the Supreme Court, displaying admirable courage and sensitivity, had quashed the 'dim-witted' law, lawyer Sunil Fernandes added that politicians haven't let go; they are still trying to discover ingenious ways to circumvent the Supreme Court's order.

The issue still remains inconclusive. The last word is yet to come, but definitely a ban is not the answer. The ban on bar dancing causes more problems than it solves.

12

LGBT Rights

Proud and Gay

'Like being a woman, like being a racial, religious, tribal, or ethnic minority, being LGBT does not make you less human. And that is why gay rights are human rights, and human rights are gay rights.'

—Hillary Clinton

Aditi hung herself from the ceiling when she discovered that her neighbour Sheetal had consumed a disinfectant. She was rushed to the hospital and survived. The incident occurred in the residential area of Chunabhatti in Mumbai. The women were in a relationship and took this extreme step after they were forbidden from seeing each other. Sheetal's father had strongly objected to their relationship and was booked for abetment of suicide and criminal intimidation.[1]

Such instances of young men and women in same-sex relationships being harassed by their parents, communities and the police are alarmingly common.

In 2001, in Kerala, two tribal girls were found dead near an irrigation canal after their families refused to let them marry. In 2008, in Chennai, two women set themselves on fire after their families tried to separate them. In 2011, in Nandigram in West Bengal, two women killed themselves, stating in their suicide note that they could not live without one another. In 2013, two young women fled to Bengaluru from Kerala, hoping to find acceptance and live together away from their disapproving families. But the father of one of them filed a kidnapping case against the other. The women then approached Sangama, a support group that works for the rights of sexual minorities in Bengaluru.

The death of a professor at the Aligarh Muslim University is another unfortunate story. In April 2010, Professor Shrinivas Ramachandra Siras, the award-winning poet who taught Marathi, was found dead under mysterious circumstances after he was suspended by the university for being gay. He was filmed participating in a homosexual act, which was consensual and took place at his private residence, with a rickshaw puller. It was perhaps shame and humiliation that drove Siras to commit suicide—that too during the period when homosexuality was decriminalized by the Delhi High Court in 2009. The movie *Aligarh* depicts his plight, with Bollywood actor Manoj Bajpayee brilliantly portraying the heartbroken professor and his trauma.

Thousands of Sirases face such intrusion into their private space and are often subjected to harassment and torture. Today, Siras symbolizes the collective cause of gay rights, the gay community's struggle to find a respectful place in society.

His death is a reminder to accept these identities and the people who are struggling to gain a foothold in society, and also help them integrate into mainstream society. 'For every such case, there might be several others that don't come to light,' says Manohar Elavarthi, founder of Sangama.

Since March 2014, the LGBT (lesbian, gay, bisexual and transgender) rights group Humsafar Trust has dealt with twelve cases in Mumbai alone where couples were either contemplating suicide or were deeply depressed or had faced some kind of harassment or coercion by family or neighbours over their sexuality.

'This is a large number and the nature of these cases is very worrying,' said Koninika Roy, advocacy manager, Humsafar Trust. 'The reaction of parents in such cases is shocking. It is harrowing to hear the women speak. They are full of guilt and they want understanding from their families, but they don't get it.'[2]

Deepa Vasudevan, founder-member of Sahayatrika, who had compiled data on the number of women in same-sex relationships who had committed suicide in Kerala, said that a majority of such cases involve young women from lower-middle-class backgrounds or small towns faced with the pressure to marry a man or forced to separate from their partners. 'What's distressing is that there is more awareness now but this is still happening,' she said.

In India, queer men and women do not have the law on their side. Section 377 of the IPC criminalizes sexual acts considered 'against the order of nature'.

Queer people are more likely to be prone to depression

and suicidal tendencies. In order to bring about acceptance, there should be support and counselling for parents of queer people—an area in which India is sorely lacking.

'It is very important to have a support mechanism for parents,' said Sonal Giani, founder of Umang, a support group for lesbians, bisexual women and transgenders. 'They are frightened of the social situation they will have to face ... Since the situation is more restrictive for women and family policing is higher, women often end up taking drastic steps.'[3]

LGBTs are merely seeking their right to equality, their right not to be criminalized for being who they are. According to senior counsel Shyam Divan, who represents Voices against 377 in the Supreme Court, 'The Constitution does not deny any citizen the right to fully develop relationships with other persons of the same gender by casting a shadow of criminality on such sexual relationships.' Yet, the LGBT community's struggle continues, and they are often subjected to arbitrary arrest, illegal detention and custodial torture by the police. Section 377 of the IPC, 1860, a colonial-era provision criminalizing consensual sexual acts of LGBT adults in private, empowered the police to arrest members of this community. According to Section 377, whoever voluntarily has carnal intercourse against the order of nature with any man, woman or animal commits an unnatural offence. This was a major hurdle for LGBTs. The section treated homosexual intercourse as a criminal offence.

The section also served as a weapon for police abuse in the form of detention, questioning, extortion, harassment, forced sex and the payment of hush money; it also perpetuated negative and discriminatory beliefs about same-sex relations and sexual minorities in general.

In a democratic country like India, shouldn't people have the right to have sex according to their dispositions? In 2009, a landmark judgment changed the status quo.

The genesis of this case went back to 2001 when the Naz Foundation (India) Trust, an NGO working in the field of HIV/AIDS intervention and prevention, moved the Delhi High Court, challenging the constitutional validity of Section 377. It did so on the grounds that the section criminalized consensual sexual acts between adults in private, and was therefore violative of Articles 21 ('Protection of Life and Personal Liberty'), 14 ('Equality before Law') and 15 ('Prohibition of Discrimination on Grounds of any Religion, Race, Caste, Sex, Place of Birth') of the Constitution.

While the high court initially refused to consider the PIL on the grounds that the NGO had no locus standi (the right to challenge or to appear in a court) in the matter, it reconsidered the issue on the Supreme Court's directions in 2004.

The Naz Foundation said that its efforts were severely impaired by the discriminatory attitudes exhibited by state authorities towards sexual minorities, men who have sex with men (MSM), lesbians and transgender individuals. The organization further stated that their self-respect and dignity could only be restored by doing away with discriminatory laws such as the one prescribed by Section 377.

It also sought to restrain the National Capital Territory of Delhi and the commissioner of police, Delhi, from enforcing the provisions in respect to sexual acts in private between consenting adults.

The National AIDS Control Association (NACO), the nodal body on HIV/AIDS-related government programmes that functions under the Union Ministry of Health and Family Welfare, too supported the cause. It said that the enforcement of the legal provision adversely contributed to pushing the HIV/AIDS infection underground, thereby making risky sexual practices go unnoticed and unaddressed. NACO stated the following in its affidavit:

> The fear of harassment by law enforcement agencies leads to sex being hurried, leaving partners without the option to consider or negotiate safer sex practices. The hidden nature of MSM groups further leads to poor access to condoms, healthcare services and safe sex information. This constantly inhibits/impedes interventions under the National AIDS Control Programme aimed at preventing spread of HIV/AIDS by promoting safe sexual practices.

Voices against 377, another LGBT coalition based in Delhi, and women's and human rights activists, too intervened to support the demand to 'read down' the provision to exclude adult consensual sex from within its purview.

According to the petitioners, the provision to penalize sexual acts, which are 'against the order of nature', was based on traditional Judeo-Christian moral and ethical standards to legitimize discrimination against sexual minorities, but it did not enjoy justification in contemporary Indian society. The section's historic and moral underpinning did not resonate with the historically held values in Indian society concerning sexual relations, they added.

Citing the 172nd report of the Law Commission, which also recommended the deletion of Section 377, the PILs stated that the provision was detrimental to people's lives and an impediment to public health due to its direct impact on the lives of homosexuals. The evidence that refuted the assumption that non-procreative sexual acts are unnatural included socio-scientific and anthropological evidence and also the natural presence of homosexuality in society at large.

The petitioners' contention was also that private, consensual sexual relations were protected under the right to liberty as enshrined in Article 21 of the Constitution. Besides, they pleaded that Section 377 was not a valid law because there existed no compelling state interest to justify the curtailment of an important fundamental freedom. Section 377, which criminalizes consensual, non-procreative sexual relations, was unreasonable and arbitrary and, therefore, violative of Articles 14 and 15 of the Constitution, the report said.

The Ministry of Home Affairs opposed the petitions on the ground that Section 377 did not suffer from any constitutional imperfection/infirmity and was not violative of fundamental rights. It said that an unlawful act cannot be rendered legitimate because the person to whose detriment it acts consents to it, adding further that there were no instances of arbitrary use of the provision. The government said that Section 377 provided a punishment for unnatural sexual offences or carnal intercourse against the order of nature. The government did not make any distinction between procreative and non-procreative sex.

The Delhi High Court Verdict

After rigorous debate went on for months together, the Delhi High Court finally allowed the PILs on 2 July 2009 and declared Section 377 and other legal prohibitions against same-sex conduct to be in direct violation of the fundamental right to life and liberty and the right to equality as guaranteed in the Constitution.

In a landmark judgment, a bench comprising Chief Justice Ajit Prakash Shah and Justice S. Muralidhar recognized the inherent injustice in Section 377's operation and struck down the provision of the Indian Penal Code. The judgment also held that 'sexual orientation is a ground analogous to sex, and that discrimination on sexual orientation is not permitted under Article 15'.

The judges clarified that 'the provisions of Section 377 will continue to govern non-consensual penile non-vaginal sex and penile non-vaginal sex and sexual acts by adults with minors'. By adult they meant 'everyone who is 18 years of age and above'.

The bench further said that 'this clarification will hold till, of course, Parliament chooses to amend the law to effectuate the recommendation of the Law Commission of India in its 172nd Report which, we believe, removes a great deal of confusion'.

The court located the rights to dignity, autonomy and privacy within the right to life and liberty guaranteed by Article 21 of the Constitution, and also held that Section 377 offended the guarantee of equality enshrined in Article 14 because it created an unreasonable classification and targeted homosexuals as a class.

While doing so, the judges referred to Indian and foreign judgments, the literature and international understanding (Yogyakarta Principles) relating to sexuality as a form of identity and the global trends in the protection of privacy and dignity rights of homosexuals.

The day the judgment was delivered, the court filled with cheers. People present in the courtroom praised the judgment and greeted one another with hugs. The high court decision was appreciated by many. Anjali Gopalan, the executive director and founder of the Naz Foundation, termed it as 'a first major step ... there are many more battles'.

'Homosexuals in the country now have the right to live like any other citizen and without being treated like criminals,' she said, but cautioned that the 'judgment didn't mean that homosexuality is legal, but that adults in [a] consensual homosexual relationship cannot be discriminated against'. Pawan Dhall, the director of Solidarity and Action against the HIV Infection in India, a Kolkata-based NGO, added, 'Personally it's a feeling of lightness, as if a huge burden has gone off my shoulders.'

However, the celebrations were short-lived. The judgment was condemned and criticized by several institutions and individuals. Several religious organizations expressed their disapproval.

Threatening to launch an all-India campaign against such tendencies, the religious leaders called upon the people who 'believe in ethical, cultural and religious values' to stand up against a calculated effort by some groups to impose upon India the 'corrupt' western value system to spoil the family system and social fabric of the country.

'This is wrong. The decision to bring Western culture to India will corrupt Indian boys and girls,' said Maulana Abdul Khaliq Madrasi, the vice chancellor of Darul Uloom, a university for Islamic education in India.

The All India Muslim Personal Law Board (AIMPLB) termed the Delhi High Court's verdict decriminalizing homosexual acts among consenting adults as 'illegal, irreligious and unnatural' for the society. It said that the court's decision was in favour of only a very small gay community. 'If legalised, these acts, which are contrary to religion, nature, morality and habits, will poison the Indian society,' the board added, while demanding that the government intervene in the matter and declare in clear terms that unnatural sex was 'unacceptable' and 'illegal'.[4]

The high court's decision should be overturned, said Dr Murli Manohar Joshi, the leader of the main Opposition party, the Hindu nationalist BJP. 'The High Court cannot decide all things,' he said.[5] Now that the high court has ruled against Section 377, some said the next step was a change in the way that society views gay people.

The then Union law minister Veerappa Moily also opposed the repealing of the provision on moral grounds, citing that the country was not yet ready for it, and advocated retaining it to avoid 'far reaching consequences'.[6]

In a united voice, almost everyone said that individuals prone to 'perverted behaviours' needed counselling and treatment, and that instead of being harassed, they should be given all possible help to overcome the unnatural tendencies.

The Supreme Court Proceedings

One Suresh Kumar Koushal, an astrologer and a yoga guru, became the first one to move the Supreme Court against the high court ruling, claiming that India's ancient scriptures and values do not permit homosexuality; decriminalizing consensual sex between persons of the same sex would lead to the spread of HIV/AIDS and 'give rise to male prostitution'.

The brigade of senior lawyers who contested the high court judgment included Amarendra Sharan, K. Radhakrishnan, V. Giri, Additional Solicitor General P.P. Malhotra, Sushil Kumar Jain, etc.

In the opening arguments, Sharan said that the impugned provision did not target any class, but applied equally to both men and women who indulge in carnal intercourse, which is against the order of nature. Thus the finding of the high court that this law offended Article 14 as it targeted a particular community known as homosexuals or gays was without any basis.

Supporting Sharan's stand, Radhakrishnan and Giri further told the court that Section 377 was enacted by the legislature to protect social values and morals and the provision did not classify people into groups, but only described it as an offence.

'What has been criminalized by Section 377 IPC is just the act, independent of the sex of people or sexual orientation,' they said, adding that same-sex intercourse is more hazardous for public health than heterosexual intercourse.

They were also joined by Jain, who contended that the high court was unjustified in striking down the provision, but should have left it to the Parliament to decide as to what is moral and what is immoral and whether the impugned section should be retained in the statute book. The 'mere possibility of abuse of any particular provision cannot be a ground for declaring it unconstitutional,' Jain contended.

However, the government did not have a unanimous stand. While the home ministry opposed the high court decision, the health ministry took a contrary stand.

Opposing the decriminalization of homosexuality, the home ministry through Additional Solicitor General P.P. Malhotra argued that the legislature, which represented the will of the people, had decided not to delete the section and that it was not for the court to import extraordinary moral values and thrust the same upon society:

> The Parliament has not thought it proper to delete or amend Section 377 IPC and there is no warrant for the HC to have declared the provision as ultra vires Articles 14, 15 and 21 of the Constitution. Every legislation enacted by Parliament or State Legislature carried with it a presumption of constitutionality. This is founded on the premise that the legislature, being a representative body of the people and accountable to them is aware of their needs and acts in their best interest within the confines of the Constitution.

Malhotra also apprised the judges about the Law Commission's 42nd report, which had recommended the retention of Section 377 of the IPC because the societal disapproval thereof was very strong.

However, the Ministry of Health and Family Welfare took a divergent view. Additional Solicitor General Mohan Jain submitted that because of their risky sexual behaviour, MSM (men who have sex with men) and female sex workers are at a higher risk of getting HIV/AIDS.

The Delhi Commission for Protection of Child Rights, the All-India Muslim Personal Law Board and the Apostolic Churches Alliance also opposed the high court judgment.

Senior advocate F.S. Nariman led arguments for campaigners fighting for the cause. The noted lawyer, who appeared for the parents of LGBT children, argued that when the sexual act is committed in private by two consenting males, for example, and not one, it cannot be regarded as an offence. The act in itself did not cause harm to either one of the two individuals indulging in it and there was mutual consent.

Senior counsel Shyam Divan said that it was scientifically established that consensual same-sex conduct is not 'against the order of nature'.

Referring to the constitutional assembly debates on Article 15 to show that the inclusion of sexual orientation in the term 'sex' was not contemplated by the founding fathers, senior counsel Huzefa Ahmadi submitted that the right to sexual orientation could always be restricted on the principles of morality and health. He also referred to the dissenting opinion given by a few judges in another case wherein it was stated that the promotion of majoritarian sexual morality was a legitimate state interest.

Another senior counsel Anand Grover told the court

that the history of unnatural offences against the order of nature and their enforcement in India during the Mughal and British times and post-Independence showed that the concept was first introduced by the British and there was no law criminalizing such acts in India.

While the privacy of heterosexual relations, especially marriage, was clothed in legitimacy, homosexual relations are subjected to societal disapproval and scrutiny, he added. The section has been interpreted to limit its application to same-sex sexual acts.

Noted film director Shyam Benegal, represented by senior lawyer Ashok Desai, argued that Section 377 of the IPC, which is a pre-Constitution statute, should be interpreted in a manner which may ensure protection of the freedom and dignity of the individuals and the court should also take cognizance of changing values. He emphasized that the attitude of the society is fast changing and the acts that were treated as offences should no longer be made punitive. He referred to medical literature to show that sexuality is a human condition and argued that it should not be regarded as a depravity or a sin or a crime so as to stigmatize homosexuality. The section stigmatized not just homosexuals but also their families. Veteran lawyer Ram Jethmalani also supported the cause, not by arguing before the apex court but through his written submissions.

The Supreme Court Verdict

On 11 December 2013, the Supreme Court dealt a severe blow to gay rights activists by overruling the historic and globally hailed verdict of the Delhi High Court. It held that homosexuality or unnatural sex between two consenting adults under Section 377 was illegal and would continue to be an offence. This provision did not suffer from any constitutional infirmity, the apex court said.

A bench comprising justices G.S. Singhvi and S.J. Mukhopadhaya set aside the Delhi High Court's verdict decriminalizing homosexuality. It, however, further said, 'Notwithstanding this verdict, the competent legislature shall be free to consider the desirability and propriety of deleting Section 377 from the statute book or amend it as per the suggestion made by Attorney-General G.E. Vahanvati.'

In the written judgment, Justice Singhvi (who retired on the same day) said:

Those who indulge in carnal intercourse in the ordinary course and those who indulge in carnal intercourse against the order of nature constitute different classes; and the people falling in the latter category cannot claim that Section 377 suffers from the vice of arbitrariness and irrational classification. What Section 377 does is merely to define the particular offence and prescribe punishment for the same which can be awarded if, in the trial conducted in accordance with the provisions of the Code of Criminal Procedure and other statutes of the same family, the person is found guilty. Therefore, the HC was not right in declaring Section 377 ultra vires Articles 14 and 15 of the Constitution.

The apex court further said:

The HC while reading down Section 377 overlooked that a miniscule fraction of the country's population constituted lesbians, gays, bisexuals or transgenders, and in the more than 150 years past, less than 200 persons were prosecuted for committing offence under this provision, and this cannot be made a sound basis for declaring that Section ultra vires Articles 14, 15 and 21.

If a provision of law was misused and subjected to the abuse of the process of law, it was for the legislature to amend, modify or repeal it, if deemed necessary, the court said.

After the review petitions were dismissed by the apex court on 28 January 2014, a batch of eight curative petitions were filed in March 2014 by parents, civil society, and scientific and LGBT rights organizations.

On 2 February 2016, the Supreme Court realized the need to revisit its earlier decision. It referred the batch of curative petitions against Section 377 to a five-judge Constitution bench for an in-depth hearing.

A three-judge bench comprising Chief Justice T.S. Thakur and justices Anil R. Dave and J.S. Khehar gave credence to the arguments that the threat imposed by the provision amounted to the denial of the rights to privacy and dignity and resulted in the gross miscarriage of justice.

A curative petition, which is filed after the dismissal of an appeal, is the last judicial resort available to redress grievances in court. It is normally decided by judges in chambers, but in this case the court agreed to give an open-court hearing.

Rebelling against the court's procedural conventions in dealing with curative pleas, Thakur said the petitions posed several questions with 'constitutional dimensions of importance'.

There was a galaxy of senior lawyers representing the petitioners, including senior advocates K.K. Venugopal, Ashok Desai, Shyam Divan, Anand Grover and Colin Gonsalves.

The decision to reopen the case came after senior advocate and former law minister Kapil Sibal told the bench that a person's sexuality was his or her most precious, most private of rights. 'Any provision that penalises an adult person's expression of consensual sexuality in private is significantly unconstitutional,' he added. 'Your past judgments not only affect the present but will bind future generations to a life of indignity and stigma . . . If not corrected now, your verdicts may result in immense public injury,' he argued.

Another petition filed by some prominent gay personalities—celebrity chef and restaurateur Ritu Dalmia, hotelier Aman Nath and dancer N.S. Johar, among others— asked the apex court to examine all over again a plea against the validity of Section 377, which makes homosexuality a criminal offence punishable with a sentence up to life imprisonment.

Stating that they are 'highly accomplished professionals', it said, 'Despite their achievements and contributions . . . they are being denied the right to sexuality, the most basic and inherent of fundamental rights. Section 377 renders them criminals in their own country.'

The Supreme Court judgment stood in place for now. This once again put the law in direct conflict with the fundamental rights of the LGBT community.

Gender rights activists felt that the apex court had missed

an opportunity to interpret fundamental rights in an expansive and purposive manner so as to enhance the dignity of the individual and the worth of the human person. Instead, it restored Section 377 to its archaic ingloriousness, validating the state's ability to criminalize acts based on perceived moral grounds, notwithstanding the effect that such laws might have on the fundamental right of a person to be treated with equal concern. It reverted to a restrictive reading of the law.

'[Stating that the] LGBT community is only a "miniscule fraction of the country's population" thereby [implies] that they are not in need of protection from the law. This is counterintuitive to the notion of discrete and insular minorities who are unable to fend for themselves,' said Siddharth Narrain, a legal and gender studies expert.

The judgment was an abdication of the Supreme Court's responsibility to safeguard the fundamental rights of all citizens, according to activists, adding that even 'a majoritarian Parliament does not want to decriminalize homosexuality. When Member of Parliament and Congress leader Shashi Tharoor brought in a private member's bill to read down Section 377, his colleagues jeered loudly at him, wondering if he needed homosexuality decriminalised for himself.'[7]

Criminalization has created a culture of silence and intolerance in society and has also perpetuated stigma and discrimination against homosexuals, who are reluctant to reveal their orientation to their family. Those who reveal their orientation are faced with shock, denial, rejection and abuse.

Legal experts feel that India in its ancient past was accommodating, if not accepting, of homosexual relations.

India's colonization by the British led to Victorian values being superimposed on what appeared to be a far more liberal and progressive society than Victorian Britain was at that time. In the words of Supreme Court lawyer Saurab Kirpal:

> The emphasis on considering homosexuality a blight along with the desire to be positively identified by the British rulers led to the expression of homosexuality becoming subdued in Indian society. This has led to a post-independent subcontinent that archetypically does not abhor homosexuality but has been indoctrinated to do so in the recent century or so. In Indian society the unique solution to this conundrum appears to be to tacitly allow homosexual relations to flourish so long as explicit acceptance is not demanded. In this way, India's liberality regarding homosexuality appears to be a mixed bag. India, therefore, is in the unique position of being homophobic but not being intolerant either. Perhaps, as of now, we have adopted a 'middle path' of our own.

There is a vibrant gay nightlife in metro cities such as Mumbai, Delhi, Kolkata, Chennai and Bengaluru. It is these metropolitan cities that have become the hub of the new gay culture with its urban outlook and acceptance towards homosexuality.

The struggle for LGBT rights in India is a relatively recent battle that has galvanized support from a wide spectrum of people across ideological boundaries, and has cut across the barriers of age, language and class. The colourful and joyous LGBT pride marches, its flamboyant imagery and the determination and enthusiasm with which this battle has been waged have won over the minds and hearts of many.

The high court judgment brought about a sea change in the mindset of the LGBT community as well as the public at large. Whereas before the judgment, the pride marches in India were poorly and thinly attended because of fear of intimidation, the marches after the judgment saw a surge in numbers. The community felt empowered and found that it could voice its ideas and concerns without the Damocles sword of prosecution hanging over their head. The reports of homosexual individuals and gatherings being harassed by the police have seen a gradual decline since 2004.

The gay pride parade is an occasion to celebrate the freedom to be who you are and feel proud of the sexual orientation you are born with. The Mumbai Gay Pride, started almost a decade ago, is the largest pride in India. Around 10,000 people participated in the parade in January 2017. It started from the August Kranti Maidan, where the Quit India Movement had begun in 1942, signifying freedom for the LGBT rights movement in India.

It remains to be seen if the Supreme Court, when addressing the curative petition, will take the courageous step of correcting the anomaly and address the gross miscarriage of justice. It can also help usher India into a more egalitarian future where LGBTs are treated as equal members of society and are allowed the right to enjoy the Constitution's foundational liberties.

'As the guardian of the Constitution that gives all Indians fundamental rights of life, dignity and privacy, the Supreme

Court must ask itself if it is doing justice to sexual minorities,' said Narrain.[8]

Lawyer Saurab Kirpal agreed that the Supreme Court in 2013 had misunderstood the role of a judge in our constitutional democracy. According to him:

> Regardless of what Parliament may or may not do, it is the Constitutional duty and responsibility of judges to uphold the values implicit in that document. They cannot shirk their responsibility to safeguard the rights of a minority by saying that the majority (i.e. Parliament) is the correct forum to protect those rights. This defeats the very purpose of embodying fundamental rights of minorities in the Constitution.

But whichever way the Supreme Court goes now, the gains made by the LGBT movement cannot be reversed that easily. Thousands of people continue to come out every day, and law or no law, there is no way that LGBT persons can be forced back into the closet. The verdict in Suresh Kumar Koushal's case may be the law today, but it is the spirit of the Naz Foundation that will stand the test of time.

Notes

Introduction

1. Shruti Singh, 'The Babri Masjid Case Timeline: What Happened and When', *India Today*, 19 April 2017.

1. The Parliament Attack

1. Dhananjay Mahapatra, 'Defending Geelani Almost Cost Me My Political Career: Jethmalani', *Times of India*, 23 November 2011, http://bit.ly/2AEJZqJ.
2. Vishwa Mohan, Bharti Jain and Indrani Basu, 'Afzal Guru Hanged, Remains in Tihar; No Last Wish, Refused to Eat', *Times of India*, 10 February 2013, http://bit.ly/2zWGCP2.
3. Rakhi Chakrabarty, 'Activists Condemn Afzal Guru's Hanging', *Times of India*, 10 February 2013, http://bit.ly/2zAiZv1.
4. Sana Shakil, 'Justice Dhingra Slams Govt over Delay in Afzal Guru's Execution', *India Today*, 10 February 2013, http://bit.ly/2yAhd9c.
5. Matthias Williams, 'Protests Erupt as India Executes Man for 2001 Parliament Attack', Reuters, 9 February 2013, http://reut.rs/2iSKchS.

6. Nandita Haksar, 'Why Afzal Must Not Be Hanged', *Mainstream Weekly*, Vol XLVIII, No 22, 22 May 2010.
7. *Shankar Kisanrao Khade v. State of Maharashtra* (2013) 5 SCC 546.
8. 'Lethal Lottery: The Death Penalty in India, A Study of Supreme Court Judgments in Death Penalty Cases 1950-2006', Amnesty International India and the People's Union for Civil Liberties (Tamil Nadu & Puducherry), 2 May 2008.

2. Nirbhaya

1. NDTV, 'Delhi Gang-Rape Verdict: Death Sentence Will Act as a Deterrant, Says Home Minister Sushil Kumar Shinde', 13 September 2013, http://bit.ly/2yZW5O8.
2. Asian News International, 'Nirbhaya Verdict Is a Reminder to Sexual Predators: Congress', 5 May 2017, http://bit.ly/2yZNECA.
3. BBC, 'Delhi Bus Gang Rape: Uproar in Indian Parliament', 18 December 2012, http://bbc.in/2hyDUHD.
4. Crime Scene Database, The Delhi Bus Gang Rape, 12 April 2016, http://crimescenedb.com/the-delhi-bus-gang-rape/.
5. *Guardian*, 'Delhi Rape Victim's Parents Call for Her Real Name to be Used to End Stigma', 16 February 2017, http://bit.ly/2hw1ZyO.

3. The 26/11 Mumbai Attacks

1. *Indian Express*, '26/11 Mumbai Terror Attacks: Here's What Happened at Taj Mahal Hotel, Trident-Oberoi, Nariman House', 3 November 2016, http://bit.ly/2AGSwcT.
2. Maitri Porecha, '26/11 Mumbai Terror Attack: Wife, Son of Victim Continue to Battle Mental Illness', *DNA*, 26 November 2016, http://bit.ly/2zVwaHz.

3. Press Trust of India, "'My Son Got Bullet for a Glass of Water'", Recalls 26/11 Victim', *The Hindu*, 29 April 2010, http://bit.ly/2idAPKn.
4. A. Ganesh Nadar, 'The Police Driver Who Died That Night', Rediff.com, 21 January 2009, http://bit.ly/2zGemiD.
5. A. Ganesh Nadar, 'The Man Who Caught Ajmal Kasab Alive', Rediff.com, 21 November 2012, http://bit.ly/2zzfQeV.
6. Rajeev Khanna, 'He Had Always Wanted to Die a Hero's Death', *Indian Express*, 30 November 2008, http://bit.ly/2AHFbAT.
7. As provided under Article 22 (1) of the Constitution.
8. As stipulated by Article 20 (3) of the Constitution.
9. *Outlook*, '26/11: Kasab's Counsel Bows to Apex Court Verdict', 29 August 2012, http://bit.ly/2zAFKPh.
10. Asseem Shaikh, Mihir Tanksale and Umesh Isalkar, 'Ajmal Kasab Sang in Cell the Night Before', *Times of India*, 22 November 2012, http://bit.ly/2AHw3fw.
11. Press Trust of India, 'Kasab's Lawyers Welcome Execution; Question the Strict Secrecy', *Deccan Herald*, 21 November 2012, http://bit.ly/2jpE8BI.
12. Asian News International, 'Girl Who Identified Kasab, Says 26/11 Mastermind Should Be Hanged', Zee News, 9 February 2016, http://bit.ly/2zI9ZS4.
13. Press Trust of India, 'What Pak Media Says on Kasab Verdict', NDTV, 4 May 2010, http://bit.ly/2hsvf68.
14. Express Web Desk, '26/11 Mumbai Terror Attacks: Here's What Happened at Taj Mahal Hotel, Trident-Oberoi, Nariman House', *Indian Express*, 3 November 2016, http://bit.ly/2AGSwcT/.
15. Barney Henderson and Amrita Kadam, 'Mumbai 26/11: Five Years On, City Still Feels Scars of Devastating Terrorist Attack', *Telegraph*, 26 November 2013, http://bit.ly/2mnIWIS.

---

4. The Babri Masjid Demolition

1. Ashish Tripathi, 'Kalyan Singh Owns Responsibility for Babri Masjid Demolition', *Times of India*, 27 October 2012, http://bit.ly/2AIlusM.
2. *Indian Express*, 'Temple Rerun: Tracing Ram Rath Yatra, 25 Years Later', 27 September 2015, http://bit.ly/2AEo7Li.
3. Dhananjay Mahapatra, 'How the Lord Became a Litigant', *Times of India*, 1 October 2010, http://bit.ly/2hsoMIt.
4. NDTV, 'Ayodhya Verdict: Allahabad High Court Says Divide Land in 3 Ways', 1 October 2010, http://bit.ly/2zGeVcf.
5. NDTV, 'Advani: A New Chapter of National Integration', 30 September 2010, http://bit.ly/2ieRX2u.
6. Ibid.
7. Vidya Subramanian, 'Babri Masjid Demolition Was Planned: Liberhan', *The Hindu*, 17 December 2016, http://bit.ly/2zD13zU.
8. *Hindustan Times*, 'Will Sacrifice Life for Ram Temple, Won't Quit as Minister: Uma Bharti on Babri Mosque Case', 24 November 2009, http://bit.ly/2icJzR2.

5. 'None of the Above'

1. Rules 41(2), (3) and 49-O of the Conduct of Election Rules, 1961.
2. Section 79(d).
3. Press Trust of India, 'Advani Endorses Narendra Modi's View on Compulsory Voting', *Indian Express*, 6 October 2013, http://bit.ly/2mor3JV.
4. *Hindustan Times*, '10 Things to Know about NOTA—A Voter's Right to Reject', 14 May 2014, http://bit.ly/2ieatro.
5. Pathikrit Chakraborty, 'UP Polls: On 12 Seats, NOTA More Than Victory Margin', *Times of India*, 13 March 2017, http://bit.ly/2iTJTDG.

6. The Uphaar Tragedy

1. Pritha Chatterjee, 'A Basement with Charred Cars, a Hall without Light for 18 Years', *Indian Express*, 20 August 2015, http://bit.ly/2zK41QR.
2. Neelam Krishnamoorthy, 'Uphaar Judgment: Had I known, I'd Have Picked up a Gun', 28 August 2015, http://bit.ly/2zBpWvK.
3. CNBC-TV18, 'Uphaar: A Case of Justice Delayed & Denied?', 16 November 2015, http://bit.ly/2iUZkvr.
4. Abhinav Garg, 'Don't Accept Rs 60 Crores: Uphaar Victims' Kin to Govt', *Times of India*, 20 August 2015, http://bit.ly/2AGTJRt.

7. Defending Freedom of Speech

1. Puja Changoiwala, 'Facebook Protest: Arrested, Slapped, Girls Still in Trauma', *Hindustan Times*, 21 November 2012, http://bit.ly/2iTlxtD.
2. *India Today*, 'Anti-corruption Cartoonist Aseem Trivedi Arrested on Sedition Charges', 9 September 2012, http://bit.ly/2AF4KSC.
3. *Times of India*, 'Jadavpur University Professor Arrested over Anti-Mamata Cartoons', 13 April 2012, http://bit.ly/2zIaZ8M.
4. Saurabh Gupta, 'Arrested for Facebook Posts, They Spent 12 Days in Jail, Lost Their Air India Jobs', NDTV, 26 November 2012, http://bit.ly/2mpGqle.
5. *Hindustan Times*, 'Status Update, Jailed: People in Trouble for Their Facebook Activity', 18 March 2015, http://bit.ly/2AIqE8m.
6. *India Today*, 'Dalit Writer Arrested for Facebook Post Criticising Akhilesh's Govt for IAS Officer Durga's Suspension', 6 August 2013, http://bit.ly/2iUf01O.
7. *Hindustan Times*, 'Arrest over a Facebook Status: 7 Times People Landed in Jail for Posts against Politicians', 24 March 2017, http://bit.ly/2yAuwqt.

8. Shreya Singhal, 'Why I, Shreya Singhal, Challenged Section 66(A)', NDTV, 25 March 2015, http://bit.ly/2zGkvLs.
9. Amit Choudhary and Dhananjay Mahapatra, 'Section 66A Quashed: Citizens Can Still Be Arrested for Online Posts', *Times of India*, 25 March 2015, http://bit.ly/2hx9V2W.
10. Article 19(1)(a) of the Constitution of India.
11. Vishnu Varma, 'Interview: Victory for Free-Speech Campaigners, Says Section 66A Petitioner', *Indian Express*, 24 March 2015, http://bit.ly/2jp9ND6.
12. Choudhary and Mahapatra, 'Section 66A Quashed'.
13. Ibid.
14. Aloke Tikku, 'SC Scrapped It, but Thousands Held Last Year under Dead Cyber Law', *Hindustan Times*, 7 September 2016, http://bit.ly/2moHK7Z.
15. Suhrith Parthasarathy, 'The Judgment That Silenced Section 66A', *The Hindu*, 26 March 2015, http://bit.ly/1VUrpgR.

8. Lily Thomas v. Union of India

1. Sagnik Dutta, 'The Judgment Will Create Awareness', *Frontline*, 9 August 2013, http://bit.ly/2zBhMn0.
2. *K. Prabhakaran v. P. Jayarajan etc.* (2005) 1 SCC 754.
3. Press Trust of India, 'Jayalalithaa Found Guilty in Disproportionate Assets Case; Verdict Assigns 4-Year Jail Term, Fine of Rs 100 Crore', *Indian Express*, 27 September 2014, http://bit.ly/2mq8zse.
4. Sana Shakil, 'MBBS Admission Scam: Jailed for 4 Years, MP Rasheed Masood to Lose Seat', *Times of India*, 2 October 2013, http://bit.ly/2zIyazT.
5. Liz Mathew, 'Fodder Scam: Lalu Prasad Disqualified from Lok Sabha', Livemint, 23 October 2013, http://bit.ly/2jn5Sql.
6. Press Trust of India, 'Every Third MP in 16th Lok Sabha Has Criminal Charges: ADR Survey', *India Today*, 18 May 2014, http://bit.ly/2zHdaJC.

7. 'Lok Sabha Election Watch 2009: A Compendium of State Election Watch Reports', Association for Democratic Reforms and National Election Watch, http://adrindia.org/sites/default/files/0.10%20full%20report%2020-05-2010.pdf.
8. Dutta, 'The Judgment Will Create Awareness'.

9. The 1993 Mumbai Blasts

1. Anupama Katakam, 'On Death Row', *Frontline*, Vol. 24, Issue 15, 28 July–10 August 2007, http://bit.ly/2hxPHGs.
2. *Indian Express*, 'Yakub Memon Must Not Hang, We Brought Him Back: Key RAW Man in '07', 29 July 2015, http://bit.ly/1Kt9c9x.
3. Press Trust of India, 'Yakub Memon May Not Live to Receive His Second Masters Degree', *Indian Express*, 29 July 2015, http://bit.ly/2jrqSfB.
4. *Indian Express*, 'Yakub Abdul Razak Memon shouldn't have been hanged', http://bit.ly/2yBVyhf.
5. *Hindustan Times*, 'Yakub Memon's Hanging Sparks Debate over Death Penalty', 31 July 2015, http://bit.ly/2hxzxNk.
6. R. Jagannathan, 'Yakub Memon Hanged: Why India Still Needs Capital Punishment', Firstpost, 31 July 2015, http://bit.ly/2ieY0Ee.

10. The Transgender Agenda

1. Dipti Nagpaul D'souza, 'All You Need Is Love: Setting an Example for India's Transgender Community', *Indian Express*, 22 January 2017, http://bit.ly/2jxKxVG.
2. Under Articles 14 and 21 of the Constitution of India.
3. It is guaranteed under Article 21 of the Constitution of India.
4. With the help of lawyers associated with the movement, the court also reviewed Article 51 of the Directive Principles of State Policy

Notes

and Article 253 of the Constitution. Articles 14, 15, 16, 19(1)(a) and 21 were analysed to bring about the desired change.

5. Laxmi, R. Raj Rao and P.G. Joshi, *Me Hijra, Me Laxmi* (New Delhi: Oxford University Press, 2015).
6. Laxmi and Pooja Pande, *Red Lipstick: The Men in My Life* (Gurgaon: Penguin Random House India, 2016).
7. Anwesha Madhukalya, 'Meet Naina, The Youngest Transgender in India to Come Out', Huffington Post, 20 July 2016, http://bit.ly/2zHdNms.
8. Ibid.
9. D'souza, 'All You Need Is Love'.
10. Ogilvy, 'Transgender Movement Inspires Indian Fashion', http://www.ogilvy.com/news-views/transgender-movement-inspires-indian-fashion/.
11. 'Vicks—Generations of Care', YouTube video, 3:37, posted by Vicks India, 9 March 2017, https://www.youtube.com/watch?v=7zeeVEKaDLM.
12. Arundhati Ramanathan, 'Workplace Equality: A Distant Dream for Transgender People', Livemint, 7 July 2016, http://bit.ly/29nAUKm.
13. Shreya Ila Anasuya, 'Over Two Years After Landmark Judgment, Transgender People Are Still Struggling', Wire, 15 May 2016, http://bit.ly/2hy1EvG.
14. Ibid.

11. The Bar Dancers Case

1. Mid-Day.com, 'Mumbai Riots Left Us Homeless, Forcing Me into Dance Bars', 17 July 2013, http://bit.ly/2AEPfdX.
2. Anjum Fatehwalla, 'The Return of Tarannum, a Richest "Bar Dancer" of Mumbai', India News Network, 18 July 2013, http://bit.ly/2hpMiFI.

3. Paul Watson, 'Prostitution Beckons India's Former Bar Girls', *Los Angeles Times*, 26 March 2006, http://bit.ly/2zIlTeM.
4. Utkarsh Anand, 'SC Lifts Maharashtra Dance Bar Ban, Says It Is Unconstitutional', *Indian Express*, 16 July 2013, http://bit.ly/2AGIJnf.

12. LGBT Rights

1. Bhavya Dore, 'A Lesbian Couple's Suicide Attempt in Mumbai Is Just One Piece of a Tragic Pattern', Scroll.in, 4 September 2016, http://bit.ly/2yZPzXK.
2. Ibid.
3. Ibid.
4. Press Trust of India, 'Legalising Homosexual Acts Is Illegal and Unnatural: Muslim Law Board', *Times of India*, 8 July 2009, http://bit.ly/2hxdENY.
5. Heather Timmons and Hari Kumar, 'Indian Court Overturns Gay Sex Ban', *New York Times*, 2 July 2009, http://nyti.ms/2joVYVg.
6. Ranjita Biswas, 'Rights-India: India's Historic Gay Ruling', Inter Press Service, 3 July 2009, http://bit.ly/2zC1xGd.
7. Shivam Vij, 'Supreme Court Should Do the Right Thing: Rethink Section 377', HuffPost India, 29 January 2016, http://bit.ly/1SfhG8e.
8. Ibid.

Sources

1. The Parliament Attack

1. *State (NCT of Delhi) v. Mohd Afzal and Others*, Sessions Case No. 53/2002, FIR No. 417/2001 (Court of S.N. Dhingra, Additional Sessions Judge, New Delhi, 18 December 2002).
2. *State and Others v. Mohd. Afzal and Others*, Murder Reference No. 1/2003 and Crl. Appeal No. 43/2003, 36 of 2003, 19 of 2003, 12 of 2003, 59 of 2003, 80 of 2003 (High Court of Delhi, 29 October 2003).
3. *State (NCT of Delhi) v. Navjot Sandhu Alias Afshan Guru and Others*, (2005) 11 SCC 600, AIR 2005 SC 3820.

2. Nirbhaya

1. *State (Government of NCT of Delhi) v. Ram Singh, since deceased and Others*, Unique ID No. 02406R0020522013, SC No. 114/2013, FIR No. 413/2012 (Special Fast Track Courts, New Delhi, 10 September 2013).
2. *State (Government of NCT of Delhi) through Reference v. Ram Singh and Ors*, Death Sentence Reference No. 6/2013 (High Court Of Delhi, 13 March 2014).

3. *Mukesh v. State (NCT of Delhi)* (2017) 6 SCC 1.

3. The 26/11 Mumbai Attacks

1. *The State of Maharashtra v. Mohammed Ajmal Mohammad Amir Kasab @ Abu Mujahid and ors*, Sessions Case No. 175 of 2009 (Court of Sessions for Greater Bombay, 3/6 May 2010).
2. *The State of Maharashtra v. Mohammed Ajmal Mohammad Amir Kasab @ Abu Mujahid and ors*, Criminal Appellate Jurisdiction Confirmation Case No. 2 of 2010 (High Court of Judicature, Bombay, 21 February 2011).
3. *Mohd. Ajmal Amir Kasab v. State of Maharashtra* (2012) 9 SCC 1 (29 August 2012).

4. The Babri Masjid Demolition

1. *Dr. M. Ismail Faruqui Etc, Mohd. . . . v. Union of India and Others*, AIR 1995 SC 605 A.
2. *Gopal Singh Visharad since deceased and survived by Rajendra Singh v. Zahoor Ahmad and Others*, Other Original Suit (O.O.S.) No. 1 of 1989 (Regular Suit No. 2 of 1950) and others (High Court of Judicature at Allahabad [Lucknow Bench], 30 September 2010).

5. 'None of the Above'

1. *People's Union for Civil Liberties v. Union of India* (2013) 10 SCC 1.

6. The Uphaar Tragedy

1. Judgments of the trial court dated 20 November 2007.
2. *Sushil Ansal v. State Through CBI*, Criminal R. 238/2001 (High Court of Delhi, 11 September 2001).

3. *Assn. of Victims of Uphaar Tragedy v. Union of India and Ors* (High Court of Delhi, 24 April 2003).
4. *Gopal Ansal v. State Through CBI* (High Court of Delhi, 19 December 2008 and 4 January 2008).
5. *Sushil Ansal v. State Through CBI*, Criminal Appeal No. 597 of 2010 (Supreme Court of India, 5 March 2014 and 19 August 2015).
6. *Sushil Ansal v. State Thr. CBI*, Criminal Appeal No. 597 of 2010 (Supreme Court of India, 22 September 2015).
7. *Association of Victims of Uphaar Tragedy v. Sushil Ansal and Another*, Review Petition (Criminal) Nos. 712–14 of 2015 in Criminal Appeals Nos. 600–02 of 2010 (Supreme Court of India, 9 February 2017).

7. Defending Freedom of Speech

1. *Shreya Singhal v. Union of India* (AIR 2015 SC 1523).

8. Lily Thomas v. Union of India

1. *Lily Thomas v. Union of India* (2013) 7 SCC 653.

9. The 1993 Mumbai Blasts

1. *State of Maharashtra, through the Secretary, Home Department and Others v. Yakub Abdul Razak Memon*, Bombay Bomb Blast Case No. 1 of 1993 (Court of Special Judge Pramod Kode designated under Terrorist and Disruptive Activities [Prevention] Act, 1987, Gr. Mumbai, 12 September 2006/27 July 2007).
2. *Yakub Memon v. State of Maharashtra* (2013) 13 SCC 1 para 148, 1253.
3. *Yakub Abdul Razak Memon v. State of Maharashtra, through the*

Secretary, Home Department and Others, Writ Petition (Crl) No. 129 of 2015 (Supreme Court of India, 28 July 2015).

4. *Yakub Abdul Razak Memon v. State of Maharashtra, through the Secretary, Home Department and Others*, Writ Petition (Crl) No. 129 of 2015 (Supreme Court of India, 29 July 2015).

5. *Yakub Abdul Razak Memon v. State of Maharashtra, through the Secretary, Home Department and Others*, Writ Petition (Crl) No. 135 of 2015 (Supreme Court of India, 30 July 2015).

10. The Transgender Agenda

1. *National Legal Services Authority v. Union of India* (2014) 5 SCC 438.

11. The Bar Dancers Case

1. *Indian Hotel and Restaurants v. The State of Maharashtra*, Writ Petition No. 2450 of 2005, W.P. No. 2052 of 2005, W.P. No. 2338 of 2005 and W.P. No. 2587 of 2005 (High Court of Judicature, Bombay,12 April 2006).

2. *State of Maharashtra and Anr v. Indian Hotel and Restaurants Assn*, Civil Appeal No. 2705 of 2006 (Supreme Court of India, 16 July 2013).

3. *State of Maharashtra and Anr v. Indian Hotel and Restaurants Assn*, Writ Petition(s) (Civil) No(s). 793/2014 (Supreme Court of India, 15 October 2016).

12. LGBT Rights

1. *Naz Foundation v. Government of Nct of Delhi and Others*, Writ Petition (C) No. 7455/2001 (High Court of Delhi, 2 July 2009).

2. *Suresh Kumar Koushal v. Naz Foundation* (2014) 1 SCC 1.